LAWS AND LEGISLATION

ENERGY PROJECTS IN FEDERAL JURISDICTIONS

LAWS AND CONSIDERATIONS

LAWS AND LEGISLATION

Additional books in this series can be found on Nova's website under the Series tab.

Additional E-books in this series can be found on Nova's website under the E-book tab.

ENERGY POLICIES, POLITICS AND PRICES

Additional books in this series can be found on Nova's website under the Series tab.

Additional E-books in this series can be found on Nova's website under the E-book tab.

LAWS AND LEGISLATION

ENERGY PROJECTS IN FEDERAL JURISDICTIONS

LAWS AND CONSIDERATIONS

MICHAEL R. BRODY
EDITOR

Nova Science Publishers, Inc.
New York

For permission to use material from this book please contact us:
Telephone 631-231-7269; Fax 631-231-8175
Web Site: http://www.novapublishers.com

LIBRARY OF CONGRESS CATALOGING-IN-PUBLICATION DATA

Vann, Adam.
Energy projects in Federal jurisdictions : laws and considerations / editors, Michael R. Brody.
p. cm.
Includes index.
"CRS report for Congress prepared for members and committees of Congress."
ISBN 978-1-62100-922-1 (softcover)
1. Energy development--Law and legislation--United States. I. Brody, Michael R. II. Title.
KF2120.A25 2011
346.7304'67915--dc23

2011040281

Published by Nova Science Publishers, Inc. † New York

CONTENTS

PREFACE

Technological advancement, financial incentives, and policy concerns have driven a global expansion in the development of renewable energy resources. Recent concerns over energy supply and pricing have led some to look increasingly to federal lands as a potential energy source. Wind energy, in particular, is now often cited as the fastest-growing commercial energy source in the world. Currently, all U.S. wind energy facilities are based on land. However, multiple offshore projects have been proposed and are at various stages of the federal permitting process. This book discusses various energy projects in federal jurisdictions including wind energy and offshore oil and gas development.

Chapter 1 - A variety of interrelated statutes and agency regulations govern leasing and permitting for energy exploration and production on federal lands.[1] Generally, these projects can be divided into two categories, each of which is governed by its own set of statutes and regulations. The first category is the exploration for and production of fossil fuels, including oil, natural gas, and coal. Oil, natural gas, and coal exploration and production on federal lands are generally governed by the Mineral Lands Leasing Act of 1920 (MLA) and subsequent amendments to that act, as administered by the Bureau of Land Management (BLM), an agency that is part of the U.S. Department of the Interior (DOI). Generally, the lessee is authorized to explore for and ultimately produce oil, natural gas, or coal on federal lands in exchange for lease payments and royalties paid to the U.S. government on the production. BLM authorizes exploration activities and production activities for lessees only upon lessees' request for permission to engage in these activities on the leased land.

Chapter 2 - The development of offshore oil, gas, and other mineral resources in the United States is impacted by a number of interrelated legal regimes, including international, federal, and state laws. International law provides a framework for establishing national ownership or control of offshore areas, and domestic federal law mirrors and supplements these standards.

Chapter 3 - Technological advancement, financial incentives, and policy concerns have driven a global expansion in the development of renewable energy resources. Wind energy, in particular, is now often cited as the fastest-growing commercial energy source in the world. Currently, all U.S. wind energy facilities are based on land. However, multiple offshore projects have been proposed and are at various stages of the federal permitting process.

In: Energy Projects In Federal Jurisdictions
Editor: Michael R. Brody
ISBN: 978-1-62100-922-1

Chapter 1

ENERGY PROJECTS ON FEDERAL LANDS: LEASING AND AUTHORIZATION

Adam Vann

SUMMARY

Recent concerns over energy supply and pricing have led some to look increasingly to federal lands as a potential energy source. This report explains the legal framework for energy leasing and permitting for onshore lands subject to the control of the federal government.

The report first reviews the laws and regulations affecting leasing of federal lands for exploration and production of oil, natural gas, and coal, as well as the permits that lessees must obtain in order to explore for and produce these resources. This leasing process has evolved over the last century under the framework established by the Mineral Leasing Act of 1920 (MLA). Oil, natural gas, and coal leasing and production on federal land pursuant to this act are currently overseen by the Bureau of Land Management (BLM), an agency within the U.S. Department of the Interior (DOI). Federal lands that the area's Resource Management Plan (RMP) determines to be amenable to oil, coal, or natural gas exploration and production may be leased by BLM, so long as such activities in that area are not prohibited by statute or regulation. Such lands are usually leased to the highest bidder as determined by competitive auction. Leaseholders are generally required to pay both rental fees and royalties (a percentage of the value of produced oil, natural gas, or coal) to the U.S. government.

The report also addresses existing laws and regulations that govern the use of federal lands for renewable energy projects, including geothermal, wind, and solar energy. BLM oversees permitting for these projects. Geothermal projects are leased in accordance with the requirements of the Geothermal Steam Act of 1970. That act functions similarly to the MLA; lands that are amenable to geothermal projects are leased to the highest qualified bidder. In contrast, wind and solar projects on federal lands are not authorized by leases, but rather by obtaining a right-of-way from BLM. These rights-of-way are issued pursuant to the requirements of Title V of the Federal Land Policy and Management Act (FLPMA), and holders of these rights-of-way must make monthly rental payments to the U.S. government.

This framework provides BLM and the federal government with flexibility to use federal lands to help satisfy the nation's energy needs, while generating revenue for the federal government and also protecting environmentally sensitive areas.

INTRODUCTION

A variety of interrelated statutes and agency regulations govern leasing and permitting for energy exploration and production on federal lands.[1] Generally, these projects can be divided into two categories, each of which is governed by its own set of statutes and regulations. The first category is the exploration for and production of fossil fuels, including oil, natural gas, and coal. Oil, natural gas, and coal exploration and production on federal lands are generally governed by the Mineral Lands Leasing Act of 1920 (MLA) and subsequent amendments to that act, as administered by the Bureau of Land Management (BLM), an agency that is part of the U.S. Department of the Interior (DOI). Generally, the lessee is authorized to explore for and ultimately produce oil, natural gas, or coal on federal lands in exchange for lease payments and royalties paid to the U.S. government on the production. BLM authorizes exploration activities and production activities for lessees only upon lessees' request for permission to engage in these activities on the leased land.

The second category pertains to renewable energy projects. Under the Federal Land Policy and Management Act of 1976 (FLPMA), solar and wind projects are often undertaken pursuant to a right-of-way or similar property interest. However, geothermal energy projects are considered mineral projects and thus are leased under a separate set of laws and regulations in a manner similar to oil and natural gas project leasing.

OIL, NATURAL GAS, AND COAL EXPLORATION AND PRODUCTION ON FEDERAL LANDS

History and Background

At the start of the 20th century, private entities could explore, develop, and purchase federal lands containing fossil fuels with relative ease. Resources on these federal lands were transferred to full private ownership pursuant to the terms of the Mining Law of 1872. This process was known as "patenting." Under the patenting process, full ownership of oil lands "could be obtained for a nominal amount."[2]

However, Congress eventually decided that oil and natural gas resources on onshore federal lands should remain under federal ownership. The enactment of the MLA ended the private acquisition of title to onshore federal lands by authorizing the Secretary of the Interior to issue permits for exploration and to lease lands containing oil, coal, natural gas and other defense-related minerals.[3] The MLA thus allowed the federal government to maintain ultimate control over these federal lands while leasing them to energy companies. The first half of this report details the legal framework for this leasing process.

Federal Lands Subject to Coal, Oil Natural Gas Leasing

The MLA authorizes the Secretary of the Interior to lease virtually all onshore lands owned by the United States that contain fossil fuel deposits, with the federal government retaining title to the lands.[4] BLM is the agency tasked with leasing these subsurface mineral rights not just for the land BLM controls but also for lands controlled by other federal agencies, including those managed by the U.S. Forest Service.[5] The MLA excludes numerous categories of lands such as national parks and monuments, as well as lands in incorporated cities, towns, and villages.[6] Areas within the National Wilderness Preservation System also cannot be leased, but valid property rights that were already in existence by 1984 are preserved.[7] In addition, although BLM controls the leasing process for subsurface rights to land in the National Forest System, the Secretary of the Interior cannot issue any lease for National Forest System lands reserved from the public domain if the Secretary of Agriculture objects.[8]

The Secretary of the Interior is also authorized to withdraw federal lands so that some or all potential land uses, including use for fossil fuel exploration and production, are not permitted on those lands.[9] A withdrawal involves "withholding an area of Federal land from settlement, sale, location, or entry, under some or all of the general land laws, for the purpose of limiting activities under those laws in order to maintain other public values in the area or reserving the area for a particular public purpose or program."[10] However, limitations on the Secretary's withdrawal authority exist. For example, Congress can make withdrawals through legislation, and the Secretary may not modify or revoke a congressional withdrawal.[11]

Development of Resource Management Plans

Bureau of Land Management

According to its website, BLM administers the leasing of minerals found beneath 258 million surface acres of federal lands that it manages, 57 million surface acres where the mineral rights are federally owned but the surface is in non-federal (mostly private) ownership,[12] and approximately 385 million acres whose surfaces are managed by other federal agencies).[13] The Secretary of the Interior must develop and revise Resource Management Plans (RMPs) for the lands under its purview that consider the present and potential future uses for lands managed by BLM.[14] These RMPs serve as the initial determinant of which lands may be subject to leasing, as all activities performed on BLM lands must be consistent with the RMPs.[15]

The Secretary generally must apply "multiple use" and "sustained yield" principles when developing RMPs.[16] "Multiple use" principles require

> management of the public lands and their various resource values so that they are utilized in the combination that will best meet the present and future needs of the American people; making the most judicious use of the land for some or all of these resources or related services over areas large enough to provide sufficient latitude for periodic adjustments in use to conform to changing needs and conditions; the use of some land for less than all of the resources; a combination of

balanced and diverse resource uses that takes into account the long-term needs of future generations for renewable and non-renewable resources."[17]

"Sustained yield" requires the maintenance of "high-level annual or regular periodic output of the various renewable resources of the lands."[18] In addition, the Secretary is required to provide opportunities for the public and various levels of government to participate in the development of RMPs.[19] This can include procedures such as holding public hearings, when appropriate.[20] Regulations require the preparation of an Environmental Impact Statement (EIS) or an Environmental Assessment (EA) in accordance with the National Environmental Policy Act (NEPA)[21] when producing an RMP.[22]

U.S. Forest Service

The Forest Service manages approximately 193 million acres under the "multiple use" and "sustained yield" policies.[23] The Forest Service develops land management plans for Forest Service lands by considering the desired conditions, objectives, suitability of areas for various uses, and other criteria.[24] As with the BLM planning process, the laws governing Forest Service land management and implementation require public notification and opportunities for public participation.[25] When analyzing Forest Service lands for potential leasing, the Forest Service classifies lands into three categories:

1. lands that will be "[o]pen to development subject to the terms and conditions of the standard oil and gas lease form";
2. lands that will be "[o]pen to development but subject to constraints that will require the use of lease stipulations"; and
3. lands that will be "[c]losed to leasing, distinguishing between those areas that are being closed through exercise of management direction, and those closed by law, regulation, etc."[26]

The Forest Service must also comply with NEPA when analyzing NFS lands for potential leasing.[27] Once the Forest Service has completed its analysis of which NFS lands will be available for leasing, it notifies BLM of its decisions, and subsequently may authorize BLM to lease the lands in question.[28]

The Leasing Process: Oil and Gas

The MLA authorizes both competitive and noncompetitive leasing processes for oil and gas exploration and production. Generally, federal lands go through the competitive leasing process first, and if no bids are received, the land will be offered for noncompetitive leasing.

The process begins when BLM generates a list of lands available for competitive oil and natural gas leasing. Private entities may respond by submitting nominations for parcels to be auctioned.[29] No unit being auctioned may exceed 2,560 acres, except in Alaska, where the maximum unit acreage is 5,760 acres.[30] In addition, each unit must be "as nearly compact as possible."[31]

The Secretary must provide 45 days notice before offering federal lands for leasing, including a 30-day period for receiving public comments after notice is published in the *Federal Register*.[32]

Competitive bidding must be held on a quarterly basis in each state where federal lands are available for leasing.[33] The Secretary may also authorize additional opportunities for bidding if he considers them to be necessary.[34]

Once the public notice requirements have been satisfied, the lands are offered for competitive leasing through an oral auction.[35] A national minimum acceptable bid of $2 per acre applies to the auction.[36] Any bids for less than the national minimum bid must be rejected.[37] A competitive bid constitutes a legally binding commitment and cannot be withdrawn.[38] The MLA requires the Secretary to accept the highest bid from a responsible qualified bidder whose bid meets or exceeds the national minimum acceptable bid.[39]

The winning bidder at a competitive auction must submit the following payments on the day of sale, unless otherwise specified: (1) the minimum bid of $2 per acre; (2) the first year's rental payment; and (3) a processing fee as set forth in BLM's regulations.[40] Then, the balance of the bonus bid, if applicable, is due within 10 working days.[41] The lease is issued within 60 days of payment of the remainder of the bonus bid.[42] The lease is also conditioned upon a royalty payment of at least 12.5% in amount or value of the production that is removed or sold from the leased land,[43] unless the Secretary suspends, waives, or reduces the royalty.[44]

The Noncompetitive Leasing Process: Oil and Gas

If no bids are received at a competitive bidding auction—or if all bids submitted are for less than the national minimum acceptable bid—the land will be offered for noncompetitive leasing within 30 days.[45] This noncompetitive leasing remains available for two years after the competitive bidding auction.[46]

The first qualified person who applies for a noncompetitive lease and pays the $75 application fee is entitled to receive the lease without having to competitively bid.[47] All noncompetitive offers received during the first business day after the last day of the competitive auction are considered to have been submitted simultaneously; in such cases, a lottery determines the lease winner.[48] Unlike competitive bids, noncompetitive offers may be withdrawn by those who submitted them within 60 days of filing the offer if no lease has yet been signed on the government's behalf.[49] As with competitive leases, a noncompetitive lease is conditioned upon payment of a 12.5% royalty in amount or value of the oil or gas removed or sold from the leased land.[50] Additionally, there are minimum and maximum acreage limitations for noncompetitive leases.[51] If these criteria are met, BLM will issue the lease within 60 days of the Secretary identifying a qualified applicant.[52]

If no application for a noncompetitive lease is submitted during the two years that the land is available for noncompetitive leasing, the process for leasing the land will again be a competitive oral auction.[53]

Lease Terms and Conditions: Oil and Natural Gas

General Statutory Restrictions

In addition to the processes affecting *where* leasing can take place, general restrictions on leasing address *who* can lease, as well as *how much* land they can lease. First, federal lands containing oil and gas deposits may only be leased to U.S. citizens, associations of U.S. citizens, corporations organized under U.S. laws or the laws of any state, and municipalities.[54] In addition, citizens of a country that denies similar privileges to U.S. citizens and corporations may not control any interest in federal leases.[55] Also, no entity is permitted to own or control oil or gas leases (including options for such leases) under the MLA in excess of 246,080 acres in any one state other than Alaska.[56] Other aggregate acreage limitations include limitations pertaining to options[57] and to combined direct and associational/corporate stockholder interests.[58]

Payment Terms: Rental Fees and Royalties

Leases are conditioned upon payment to the government of a royalty of at least 12.5% in amount or value of oil or gas production that is removed or sold from the leased land.[59] The Secretary has the power to reduce the royalty rate on a noncompetitive lease if he deems it equitable to do so or if circumstances could "cause undue hardship or premature termination of production" absent such a reduction.[60] For oil and gas leases, the royalty must be paid in value unless the Department of the Interior specifies that a royalty payment-in-kind is required.[61] Once the royalty has been paid, the Secretary is required to sell any royalty oil or gas "except whenever in his judgment it is desirable to retain the same for the use of the United States."[62]

In addition to royalties, leases are conditioned upon payment of annual rental fees.[63] Generally, the rate for the first five years of a lease is $1.50 per acre per year, with the rate increasing to $2 per acre for each additional year of the lease.[64] However, there is some variation in rental fee amounts for certain categories of lands.[65] For leases issued after December 22, 1987, a minimum royalty in lieu of the rental fee is due once oil or gas has been discovered on the leased land.[66] The amount of this minimum royalty is equal to the annual rental fee that would otherwise have been due.[67] Rental payments are not due on acreage for which royalties or minimum royalties are being paid, "except on nonproducing leases when compensatory royalty has been assessed in which case annual rental as established in the lease shall be due in addition to compensatory royalty."[68]

Money received from royalties and rental fees is initially paid into the U.S. Treasury.[69] Fifty percent of the funds then go to the state where the land or mineral deposit is located.[70] Forty percent of the funds are allocated into the Reclamation Fund under the Reclamation Act of 1902 for projects that provide water to arid Western states.[71] The remaining moneys are credited to the "miscellaneous receipts."[72] Because Alaska is not served by the Reclamation Fund, 90% of the funds collected from federal leases in Alaska are allocated to the State of Alaska.[73] The Secretary is authorized to waive, suspend, or reduce rental fees and royalties under certain conditions.[74]

Lease Terms, Extensions, and Cancellations

The primary term for competitive and noncompetitive leases is 10 years.[75] Leases can be extended to allow for the continuation of exploration operations or oil or gas production. The existence of an approved cooperative plan can also affect extensions.

First, a lease will be extended for two years because of *drilling* if three criteria are satisfied:

1. actual drilling operations began before the end of the primary lease term;

2. actual drilling operations are being "diligently prosecuted" at the end of the primary lease term; and
3. rental fees were paid in a timely manner.[76]

Second, a lease that meets these criteria will be extended "so long as oil or gas is being *produced* in paying quantities."[77] A lease that has been extended because of production does not terminate when production stops, as long as the lessee starts reworking or drilling operations within 60 days after production ceases and conducts them with reasonable diligence during the non-productive period.[78] Furthermore, if a lease initially extended because of drilling begins yielding oil or gas in paying quantities during the two-year drilling extension, the lease can be extended again.[79]

Finally, lessees may collectively adopt and operate under a cooperative plan for exploration and production in a particular area if the Secretary considers such a plan to be in the public interest.[80] All leases subject to such a plan will be extended if any of the leases covered by the plan qualify for a drilling or production extension.[81]

Any MLA lease can be cancelled or forfeited if the lessee fails to comply with the statute, the lease's provisions, or regulations promulgated pursuant to MLA.[82] In some situations the Secretary has the authority to cancel the lease unilaterally, but some circumstances require a judicial proceeding to cancel the lease.[83] In addition, MLA provides for *automatic* termination "upon failure of a lessee to pay rental on or before the anniversary date of the lease, for any lease on which there is no well capable of producing oil or gas in paying quantities."[84] However, the Secretary may in some circumstances reinstate automatically terminated leases.[85]

Applications for Permits to Drill: Oil and Gas

Bureau of Land Management

Operators[86] must submit an Application for a Permit to Drill (APD) for each oil or gas well.[87] Without an approved APD, operators cannot begin drilling operations or cause surface disturbances that are preliminary to drilling.[88] In fact, the APD process must begin at least 30 days prior to the commencement of operations.[89]

A complete APD must include the following:

- a drilling plan;

- a surface use plan of operations, including drillpad locations and plans for reclaiming the surface;
- evidence of bond coverage;
- a BLM form; and
- any other information that may be required.[90]

Once BLM receives an APD, it must make available information for public inspection for at least 30 days before it may act on the APD.[91] Another pre-approval requirement is that BLM must prepare an environmental record of review or an environmental assessment.[92] Based on these documents, BLM decides whether an EIS is required.[93]

Within five working days of the end of the public notice period, BLM must choose one of four options:

1. approve the application as submitted;
2. approve the application with modifications and/or conditions;
3. disapprove the application; or
4. delay final action.[94]

BLM must also approve a surface use plan of operations addressing proposed surface-disturbing activities before a permit to drill on lands BLM manages may be granted.[95]

U.S. Forest Service

An approved surface use plan of operations addressing proposed surface-disturbing activities is also required before a permit to drill on Forest Service lands may be granted and before any surface-disturbing operations may begin.[96] The operator must submit its proposed surface use plan of operations to BLM as part of its APD.[97] When the proposal pertains to NFS lands, BLM forwards the proposed surface use plan of operations to the Forest Service for evaluation.[98]

The level of detail required in a proposed plan varies depending upon the "type, size, and intensity of the proposed operations and the sensitivity of the surface resources that will be affected by the proposed operations."[99] When evaluating a proposed surface use plan of operations, the Forest Service must ensure that the proposal is consistent with the approved forest land and resource management plan for that area of land.[100] During the evaluation process, the Forest Service must also comply with NEPA, as well as appropriate Forest Service regulations and policies.[101] In addition, the Forest

Service can require that the operator increase the amount of its bond if it "determines [that] the financial instrument held by [BLM] is not adequate to ensure complete and timely reclamation and restoration" of the NFS lands.[102]

Ultimately, the Forest Service must decide among four options:

1. approve the plan;
2. approve the plan "subject to specified conditions";
3. disapprove the plan; or
4. delay the plan because additional time is needed to reach a decision.[103]

Once it has made its decision regarding the proposed surface use plan of operations, the Forest Service forwards the decision to BLM, which conducts the leasing of the relevant land in accordance with its regulations.[104]

The Leasing Process: Coal

All BLM coal leasing is done competitively except in cases where a party holds a "prospecting permit" issued prior to the Federal Coal Leasing Amendments Act of 1976 or where contiguous lands are added to existing leases.[105] The process for coal leasing on federal lands is similar to the process for oil and gas leasing. It is governed by Section II of the MLA as amended.[106] Under the statute as amended (most significantly in the aforementioned Federal Coal Leasing Amendments Act of 1976) and the regulations adopted pursuant to it, coal leasing on federal lands may not commence until the land to be leased has been included in a comprehensive land use analysis.[107] The coal screening aspect of this analysis consists of several determinations: (1) the identification of coal-rich areas with potential for development; (2) evaluation of the land in question to determine whether there are any factors that would make it unsuitable for development; (3) consideration of potential multiple use conflicts; and (4) in cases where the federal government does not control the surface estate, consultation with the surface estate owner regarding development of coal resources.[108]

There are two processes by which federal lands may be leased for coal production. The first is "regional coal leasing," in which BLM selects tracts for leasing as needed to meet regional requirements as outlined by "regional coal teams" composed of BLM officials and interested state and local parties. The second is leasing on application.

Regional Coal Leasing

The regional coal leasing process begins with the establishment of regional coal leasing levels by the Secretary of the Interior, informed by the input of the relevant state governors and other interested parties, after consideration of a number of social, economic, and environmental factors.[109] The next step is the delineation and ranking of tracts acceptable for further consideration for coal leasing.[110] After the completing of tract ranking and selection, BLM produces a regional coal leasing environmental impact statement (EIS) to satisfy the requirements of NEPA.[111] This EIS must consider both the site-specific potential environmental impacts of each potential tract lease and the intraregional cumulative environmental impacts of the proposed leasing and alternatives.[112] After completion of the EIS, BLM will consult with any federal agencies potentially affected by the potential leasing,[113] as well as potentially affected governors and Indian tribes,[114] before adopting a regional lease sale schedule.[115]

The lease sales themselves begin with a determination of the fair market value (FMV) of the tract or tracts to be offered, along with the maximum economic recovery for the tract or tracts.[116] BLM does not accept any bid for less than the FMV as determined.[117] After notice of the lease sale is properly given, BLM fields bids and announces the highest bid, which is awarded the lease if it otherwise satisfies all applicable lessee requirements, although BLM reserves the right to reject any and all bids for any reason.[118]

Leasing on Application

BLM also conducts coal leasing in response to applications from interested parties. The process begins with the submission of an application by a qualified potential lessee to lease for purposes of coal development any BLM lands that have been included in a comprehensive coal land use plan or analysis.[119] The application must contain certain data intended to assist BLM in conducting the environmental analysis needed to satisfy the requirements of NEPA.[120] After this process is completed, BLM determines the FMV and maximum economic recovery for the proposed lease tract,[121] and consults with the same parties with whom consultation is required for regional leasing as described in the previous section of this report.[122] After these requirements are met, the lease sale is conducted in the same manner applicable to regional coal lease sales, as described in the previous section.[123]

Lease Terms and Conditions: Coal

General Statutory Restrictions

As with oil and natural gas leasing, coal tracts may only be leased to U.S. citizens, associations of U.S. citizens, corporations organized under U.S. laws or the laws of any state, and municipalities. Also, no entity is permitted to own or control coal leases with an aggregate acreage in excess of 75,000 acres in any one state or more than 150,000 acres in the United States.[124] Parties who have held a federal coal lease for 10 or more years that has not produced commercial quantities of coal may not acquire any other mineral leases under the Mineral Leasing Act of 1920, as amended.[125]

Coal Lease Terms

BLM-issued coal leases are for initial terms of 20 years, with automatic extension "for so long thereafter as coal is produced annually in commercial quantities from that lease."[126] In addition to rental payments of not less than $3 per acre,[127] lessees are required to make payment to the government of a royalty of at least 12.5% in amount or value of coal that is recovered from the leased land.[128] The Secretary has the authority to determine other applicable terms and conditions of coal leases. All leases are subject to the condition of diligent development and continued operation.[129] Lessees must also furnish bonds sufficient to ensure compliance with the terms and conditions of the lease.[130]

RENEWABLE ENERGY PROJECTS ON FEDERAL LANDS

Background

In recent years, concern over the impact of emissions from fossil fuel-fired power plants has resulted in increased interest in renewable energy sources. Because the federal government controls land in areas with topography that is considered suitable for renewable energy projects, BLM has issued leases or rights-of-way for a number of renewable energy projects. This section discusses the relevant statutes and regulations applicable to such projects.

The generally applicable requirements and restrictions for lands managed by BLM discussed previously in this report also apply to this discussion of renewable energy projects on federal lands. Renewable energy uses can be considered during the formulation of Resource Management Plans (RMPs) for federal lands. Because the energy source does not expire and because the requisite gathering facilities often leave a relatively small footprint, renewable energy can often be an attractive option when applying the "multiple use" and "sustained yield" principles during the RMP process as described *supra* in the section of this report titled "Development of Resource Management Plans."

Geothermal Project Leasing

Background

Geothermal energy is energy that is produced from heat stored under the surface of the earth. Geothermal energy is produced by releasing cold water under the surface into a "hot" area in order to generate steam to fuel the generation of power. BLM has the delegated authority to lease 247 million acres of lands in the Western United States and Alaska (including 104 million acres of lands managed by the Forest Service)[131] with geothermal potential.[132] BLM currently manages 530 geothermal energy leases, with 58 leases producing 1,275 megawatts of electricity, about half of the total amount of U.S. geothermal energy production capacity.[133]

Geothermal energy projects administered by BLM differ from most other renewable energy projects on federal lands in that they are operated pursuant to a lease, rather than a more limited authorization like a right-of-way. The governing law for steam leasing is the Geothermal Steam Act of 1970.[134] The act sets forth detailed provisions governing the issuance and administration of geothermal steam leases. The laws and regulations governing geothermal steam leasing and administration are similar to the principles and processes for oil and natural gas leasing on federal lands described in detail earlier in this report.

The Leasing Process

The Geothermal Steam Act, like the MLA, authorizes both competitive and noncompetitive leasing processes. The competitive process begins when BLM receives nominations for parcels to be auctioned from a qualified company or individual.[135] Nominated areas may not exceed 5,120 acres unless the lease area includes an irregular subdivision.[136] Qualified companies or individuals may request that nominated parcels be offered as a block for competitive leasing.[137]

The Secretary must provide 45 days notice by posting in the applicable BLM office before offering federal lands for geothermal leasing.[138] BLM must hold competitive bidding for geothermal leases at least once every two years.[139] Once the public notice requirements have been satisfied, the federal lands are offered for competitive leasing through an auction at the time, date, and place specified in the public notice.[140]

Bidders must make a minimum acceptable bid of $2 per acre for the first year, $3 per acre for years 2-10, and $5 per acre for every year after year 10 of the lease.[141] A competitive bid constitutes a legally binding commitment and cannot be withdrawn.[142] BLM will accept the highest bid from a qualified bidder.[143] The winning bidder must pay 20% of the bid amount, the total amount of the first year's rental, and a processing fee to BLM by the close of business on the day following the day of the lease sale.[144] The remainder of the bid amount must be submitted to BLM within 15 calendar days of the day of the sale.[145]

Lands offered at a competitive lease sale that receive no bids are made available for noncompetitive leasing for a two-year period beginning the first business day following the date of the lease sale.[146] For the first 30 days following the lease sale, leases are available only for parcels as configured for the lease sale; after 30 days, BLM accepts applications for any available lands covered by the lease sale.[147] Holders of mining claims on federal lands may apply for noncompetitive geothermal leases within the lands on which they hold claims.[148]

Geothermal steam project leases can also be obtained though "direct use" leasing. Direct use of geothermal energy involves the use of geothermal hot water directly for its intended end use, rather than for transfer into electricity that is then transmitted to the end user. Applicants can obtain direct use leases if (1) the lands in question are open for geothermal leasing; (2) BLM determines that the lands are appropriate for direct use operations without sale for purposes other than commercial generation of electricity; (3) BLM has published notice of the proposal to use the land for direct use leasing; (4) during the 90-day period following the publication of such notice, BLM does not receive any nomination to include the land in question in the next competitive lease sale; and (5) BLM determines there is not competitive interest in the resource.[149]

Geothermal leases generally have an initial primary term of 10 years, with a number of extensions that can extend the term at the discretion of BLM.[150] The first five-year extension is granted if the lessee has expended a minimum of $40 per acre in development activities that provide additional geologic or reservoir information.[151] Subsequent extensions may be granted upon showings of continued annual expenditures and progress in the development of geothermal resources.[152]

Lessees are required to make annual rental payments to BLM. For leases acquired in a competitive lease sale and issued on or after August 8, 2005, the annual rent is $2 per acre for the first year and $3 per acre for the second through the 10th year.[153] For leases acquired noncompetitively, the annual rent is $1 per acre for the first 10 years of the lease.[154] For both types of leases, the annual rent is $5 per acre each year after the 10th year.

Lessees must also make royalty payments on electricity produced from geothermal steam on federal lands. For leases issued on or after August 8, 2005, the royalty rate is 1.75% of gross sales for the first 10 years of production, and 3.5% thereafter.[155] If the lessee sells the geothermal resources to a third party who then uses those resources to produce electricity, the royalty rate on the sale is 10%.[156] Direct use lessees do not have to pay royalties unless they sell the geothermal steam resources to a third party; instead, they must pay a direct use fee in accordance with a published fee schedule.[157]

Geothermal leases can be suspended or cancelled at the discretion of the Secretary of the Interior. The Secretary may suspend leases in the interest of conservation of resources, and may terminate leases for any violation of the BLM regulations or the lease terms.[158] The Secretary is also authorized to waive, suspend, or reduce the rental or royalty rates for any lease in the interest of conservation.[159] The lessee may also suspend the lease on their own motion in the interest of conservation.[160]

Exploration and Production Under Geothermal Leases

As with oil and natural gas leasing, a geothermal lease alone does not entitle the lessee to commence drilling and production. In order to conduct exploration for geothermal resources, the lessee must submit to BLM a Notice of Intent to Conduct Geothermal Resource Exploration Operations.[161] Exploration operations must be conducted in a manner that (1) protects the quality of surface and subsurface waters, air, and other natural resources; (2) protects the quality of cultural, scenic, and recreational resources; (3) accommodates other land uses; and (4) minimizes noise.[162] Data collected during exploration operations must be shared with BLM.[163]

Lessees must also submit a geothermal drilling program and obtain a drilling permit before commencing drilling operations for geothermal resources on leased land.[164] Similar to exploration operations, drilling operations must be conducted in a matter that (1) protects the quality of surface and subsurface waters, air, and other natural resources; (2) protects the quality of cultural, scenic, and recreational resources; (3) accommodates other land uses; (4) minimizes noise; and (5) prevents property damage and unnecessary or undue degradation of the lands.[165] Lessees must also meet BLM's geothermal well abandonment requirements upon completion of operations.[166]

Authorizations for Wind and Solar Energy Projects

While oil, gas, and geothermal projects are permitted by BLM under leasing processes, those interested in producing wind or solar energy on federal lands do not seek leases. Instead, they seek more limited authorizations for development of their energy projects pursuant to Title V of the Federal Land Policy and Management Act (FLPMA).[167]

Background

Federal lands also have significant capacity for both wind and solar energy production. BLM manages 20.6 million acres of federal lands with wind potential in 11 Western states.[168] BLM has amended 52 different land use plans to allow for development of wind energy projects.[169] The Southwestern United States has some of the highest solar radiation levels in the world, a characteristic that makes it a possible candidate for solar energy development.[170] Because of these characteristics, BLM has been active in consideration and promotion of wind and solar energy projects on the lands that it manages.

As with oil, gas and geothermal leasing, not all federal lands are available for wind and solar renewable energy project rights-of-way. Lands designated as Wilderness Areas and Wilderness Study Areas, National Monuments, National Conservation Areas (with the notable exception of the California Desert Conservation Area), National Wild and Scenic Rivers, and National Historic and Scenic Trails, are categories of land not open to solar and wind energy development.[171] In addition, some special management areas, such as Areas of Critical Environmental Concern, may not be suitable for development.[172]

Title V of FLPMA authorizes BLM and the Secretary of Agriculture (managing Forest Service lands) to "grant, issue or renew rights-of-way over, upon, under or through" their administered lands for "systems for generation, transmission and distribution of electric energy."[173] Neither Title V of FLPMA nor the accompanying regulations address wind or solar energy projects specifically. However, because wind and solar projects on federal lands are conducted via rights-of-way, many of the provisions of FLPMA and the accompanying regulations are relevant.

The agencies may exercise their discretion to grant rights-of-way on any lands under their jurisdiction, unless (1) prohibited by a statute, regulation or order that specifically excludes rights-of-way; (2) the lands are specifically segregated or withdrawn from the use contemplated by the right-of-way; or (3) the agency has identified the area in land use plans as inappropriate for right-of-way uses.[174]

BLM Rights-of-Way

Parties applying for BLM rights-of-way for development of wind or solar energy projects must satisfy a number of requirements in their application, as set forth by the Secretary of the Interior.[175] These include disclosures regarding information related to the use of the right-of-way, information regarding the identification of business partners and other affiliated entities, and information regarding plans for use of the right-of-way.[176] Applications for rights-of-way on BLM lands must be accompanied by a processing fee as set forth in BLM regulations.[177] All filed information is kept confidential to the extent allowed by law.[178]

Rights-of-way granted by BLM function differently from leases in several respects. Perhaps the most significant difference between leases and rights-of-way are the substantial rights to use of the land in question retained by the lessor, the United States. BLM retains the right to:

1. access the lands covered by the right-of-way, including any facilities constructed on the right-of-way;
2. require common use of the land (including subsurface and air space) and to authorize others to use the right-of-way for compatible uses;
3. retain ownership of the resources of the land;
4. determine whether or not the grant is renewable; and
5. change the terms and conditions of the right-of-way as a result of changes in legislation or regulation or as otherwise necessary to protect public health or safety or the environment.[179]

BLM may also include in a right-of-way grant any terms, conditions, or stipulations that it determines to be in the public interest, including modifications of proposed routes or changes to the location of certain facilities.[180] Rights-of-way may also completely prohibit use of the land until BLM has approved a Plan of Development for the land and issued a Notice to Proceed to the right-of-way holder.[181] The terms of rights-of-way vary, but those with terms longer than 20 years must include periodic reviews at the end of the 20th year and at 10-year intervals thereafter.[182]

Holders of BLM rights-of-way are also required to make rent payments as set forth by BLM. Rent is payable on a monthly basis,[183] and waivers or reductions can be obtained.[184] BLM regulations provide that rent for non-linear rights-of-way for purposes other than communications uses will be determined through a process based on comparable commercial practices, appraisals, competitive bidding, or other reasonable methods.[185]

BLM completed a Programmatic Environmental Impact Statement (PEIS) for a wind energy permitting program in June 2005, and in 2006 issued a policy to provide guidance on best management practices to mitigate potential negative environmental impacts, including impacts on birds and wildlife habitat.[186]

BLM has published "Pre-application and Screening" guidance for wind and solar right-of-way applicants,[187] as well as guidance on the due diligence requirements these applicants must satisfy.[188] BLM continues to develop its PEIS for solar energy project licensing, and the publication of the PEIS for the program is the next significant step toward development of solar resources on federal lands.[189]

Forest Service Special Use Authorizations

The Forest Service also does not have regulations that specifically address wind and solar energy rights-of-way, so the agency would look to generally applicable laws and regulations as guidance for the authorization of wind or solar projects. The Forest Service does not currently authorize any such projects on its lands. Applicants seeking to make use of Forest Service lands for such a project would apply for "special use authorization" under the generally applicable regulations for such authorizations.

All uses of National Forest System lands other than road usage, grazing and livestock use, sale and disposal of timber and other forest products, and mineral usage are designated as "special uses."[190] Before conducting a special use on these lands, individuals or entities must submit a proposal to a Forest Service-authorized officer[191] and must obtain "special use authorization" from that authorized officer, unless that requirement is waived under regulations that are likely not applicable to energy projects.[192] Among the permitted authorizations are "permits, leases and easements ... for rights-of-way for ...

systems and related facilities for generation, transmission and distribution of electric energy,"[193] which would authorize wind or solar generation facilities.

Applicants for special use authorizations must contact the Forest Service office(s) responsible for management of the affected land as early as possible in advance of the proposed use.[194] Upon receipt, the authorized officer screens the application in two phases to ensure that the proposed use is consistent with the laws, regulations, orders, and policies establishing or governing National Forest System lands,[195] that the proposed use is consistent with the standards and guidelines in the applicable forest land and RMP,[196] that the proposed use will not create an exclusive or perpetual right of use or occupancy,[197] and that other Forest Service initial screening concerns are satisfied.[198] After this second-level screening, a formal application is submitted and processed,[199] and federal, state, and local agencies and the public are afforded the opportunity to comment on the application.[200] After review and a decision to approve, the authorized officer may issue a special use authorization.[201]

Special use authorizations are subject to a number of limitations. All rights not expressly granted are reserved to the United States, including:

1. continuing rights of access to all Forest System lands;
2. a continuing right of physical entry to any part of the authorized facilities; and
3. the right to require common use of the land or to authorize the use by others in any way not inconsistent with a holder's existing rights and privileges after consultation.[202]

A number of other mandatory terms and conditions apply to the Forest Service-issued special use authorizations, as set forth in the regulations.[203] Special use authorization holders also must pay an annual rental fee for the authorization, as determined by the authorized officer based on the fair market value of the rights and privileges authorized, as determined by appraisal or other sound business management principles.[204] The Forest Service also may collect processing fees from applicants and holders to recover its costs.[205]

The Forest Service may suspend, revoke, or terminate a special use authorization under any of the grounds articulated in its regulations.[206] The regulations do not provide specific guidance on duration and renewability of special use authorizations, providing simply that "[i]f appropriate, each special use authorization will specify its duration and renewability. The duration shall be no longer than the authorized officer determines is necessary to accomplish the purpose of the authorization and to be reasonable in light of all circumstances concerning the use."[207] Where renewal is provided for, the authorized officer will renew the authorization if the project or facility is still being used for the purpose(s) previously authorized and is being operated and maintained in accordance with all the provisions of the authorization.[208] Where no such renewal provision is in place, the authorization can be renewed at the authorized officer's discretion upon request of the holder.[209]

End Notes

[1] This report provides a discussion of energy projects on onshore federal lands (i.e., any land in which the federal government maintains a property interest). For discussion of offshore energy projects, see CRS Report RL33404, *Offshore Oil and Gas Development: Legal Framework*, by Adam Vann; CRS Report R40175, *Wind Energy: Offshore Permitting*, by Adam Vann; and CRS Report RL34741, *Drilling in the Great Lakes: Background and Issues*, coordinated by Pervaze A. Sheikh.

[2] *See* Pan Am. Petroleum & Transp. Co. v. United States, 273 U.S. 456, 486 (1927) (internal citation omitted).

[3] Mineral Lands Leasing Act of 1920 41 Stat. 4373 (1920), codified at 30 U.S.C. §181 *et seq.*

[4] 30 U.S.C. §181.

[5] *Id.*

[6] *Id.*

[7] 16 U.S.C. §1133(d)(3) ("Subject to valid rights then existing, effective January 1, 1984, the minerals in lands designated ... as wilderness areas are withdrawn from all forms of appropriation under the mining laws and from disposition under all laws pertaining to mineral leasing and all amendments thereto.").

[8] *Id.* at §226(h). In addition, the U.S. Forest Service has issued separate regulations governing certain aspects of leasing and permitting for oil and gas development on lands within its jurisdiction.

[9] 43 U.S.C. §1714 (2000).

[10] *Id.* at §1702(j).

[11] 43 U.S.C. §§1701(a)(4), 1714(j); 43 C.F.R. §2300.0-3(a).

[12] http://www.blm.gov/wo/st/en/prog/energy/oil_and_gas/leasing_of_onshore.html.

[13] *Id.* In addition to the Forest Service lands discussed in this report, the 385 million acres for which BLM would manage subsurface rights include National Park lands, lands controlled by the Fish and Wildlife Service or the Department of Defense, and other lands that are not frequently leased for development of subsurface natural resources.

[14] 43 U.S.C. §1712; 43 C.F.R. Parts 1600, 1610.

[15] 43 C.F.R. §1610.5-3.

[16] 43 U.S.C. §§1701(a)(7), 1732(a). An exception applies in circumstances "where a tract of such public land has been dedicated to specific uses according to any other provisions of law [in which case] it shall be managed in accordance with such law." 43 U.S.C. §1732(a).

[17] *Id.* at §1702(c).

[18] *Id.* at §1702(h).

[19] *Id.* at §1712(f).

[20] *Id.*

[21] 42 U.S.C. §§4321 et seq.

[22] *See* 43 C.F.R. §1601.0-6. The regulations stipulate that approval of an RMP constitutes a "major Federal action significantly affecting the quality of the human environment"; thus,

the preparation of an Environmental Impact Statement (EIS) is required pursuant to NEPA. *Id.*; *see* 42 U.S.C. §4332(2)(C). NEPA also requires BLM to take a "hard look" at the environmental impacts of significant proposed actions. 42 U.S.C. §4332(2)(C). If it is unclear whether a proposed action will have significant environmental effects, the agency may prepare an Environmental Assessment (EA). 40 C.F.R. §1501.3. Based on the EA, an agency may issue a finding of no significant impact (FONSI), thereby concluding the NEPA process, or it may determine that preparation of an EIS is necessary. *Id.* §1508.13. An EIS must address numerous issues, including the environmental impact of the proposed action, alternatives to the proposed action, and any irreversible commitments of resources which would be involved if the proposed action takes place. 42 U.S.C. §4332(2)(C). For further discussion of NEPA, see CRS Report RS20621, *Overview of National Environmental Policy Act (NEPA) Requirements*, by Kristina Alexander.

[23] Multiple-Use Sustained-Yield Act, P.L. 86-517, codified at 16 U.S.C. §§528-532.

[24] 16 U.S.C. §1604; 36 C.F.R. §§219.5, 219.7

[25] 16 U.S.C. §§1604(d), 1612; 36 C.F.R. §219.9.

[26] 36 C.F.R. §228.102(c).

[27] 16 U.S.C. §1604(g); 36 C.F.R. §228.102(a).

[28] 36 C.F.R. §228.102(d), §228.102(e).

[29] *See* 43 C.F.R. §3120.3-1.

[30] 30 U.S.C. §226(b)(1).

[31] *Id.*

[32] 30 U.S.C. §226(f).

[33] 30 U.S.C. §226(b)(1).

[34] *Id.*

[35] *Id.*

[36] 30 U.S.C. §226(b)(1)(B); 43 C.F.R. §3120.1-2.

[37] 30 U.S.C. §226(b)(1).

[38] 43 C.F.R. §3120.5-3(a).

[39] 30 U.S.C. §226(b)(1).

[40] 43 C.F.R. §3120.5-2.

[41] *Id.*

[42] 30 U.S.C. §226(b)(1).

[43] *Id.*

[44] 30 U.S.C. §209.

[45] 30 U.S.C. §226(b)(1), (c).

[46] *Id.*

[47] 30 U.S.C. §226(c)(1).

[48] 43 C.F.R. §3110.2(a).

[49] *Id.* at §3110.6.

[50] 30 U.S.C. § 226(c)(1). As mentioned above, the Secretary may suspend, waive, or reduce rentals or royalties under certain conditions. *See, e.g.*, 30 U.S.C. §209.

[51] *See* 43 C.F.R. §3110.3.

[52] 30 U.S.C. §226(c)(1).

[53] 30 U.S.C. §226(c)(2)(A).

[54] 30 U.S.C. §181.

[55] *Id.*

[56] *Id.* at §184(d)(1). For Alaska, the limit is 300,000 acres in the northern leasing district and 300,000 acres in the southern leasing district, of which no more than 200,000 acres may be held under options in each of the two leasing districts. 30 U.S.C. § 184(d).

[57] 30 U.S.C. §184(d)(2).

[58] *Id.* at §184(e)(1).

[59] *Id.* at §226(b)(1).

[60] 30 U.S.C. §188(i)(1).

[61] 30 C.F.R. §§202.100, 202.150.
[62] 30 U.S.C. §192.
[63] *Id.* at §226(d).
[64] *Id.*; 43 C.F.R. §3103.2-2(a). The rental payment for the first year of the lease must be included with each competitive bid or noncompetitive lease offer. 43 C.F.R. §3103.2-1.
[65] *See* 43 C.F.R. § 3103.2-2.
[66] *Id.* at §3103.3-2(a).
[67] *Id.*
[68] *Id.* at §3103.2-2(c).
[69] *Id.* at §191(a).
[70] *Id.*
[71] *Id.*
[72] *Id.*
[73] *Id.*
[74] *See, e.g.*, 30 U.S.C. §209.
[75] 30 U.S.C. §226(e).
[76] *Id.*; 43 C.F.R. §3107.1. Other regulations regarding the continuation, extension, and renewal of leases are set forth in 43 C.F.R. §§3107.1 *et seq*.
[77] 30 U.S.C. §226(e) (emphasis added).
[78] 30 U.S.C. §226(i); 43 C.F.R. §3107.2-2.
[79] *See* 30 U.S.C. §226(e).
[80] *Id.* at §226(m).
[81] *Id.*; 43 C.F.R. §3107.3-1.
[82] 30 U.S.C. §188(a); 43 C.F.R. §3108.3(a), (b).
[83] *See* 43 C.F.R. §3108.3(a), (b).
[84] 30 U.S.C. §188(b).
[85] *See id.* at §188(c)-(e), (g), (j).
[86] BLM Regulations define an *Operator* as "any person or entity including but not limited to the lessee or operating rights owner, who has stated in writing to the authorized officer that it is responsible under the terms and conditions of the lease for the operations conducted on the leased lands or a portion thereof." 43 C.F.R. §3160.0-5.
[87] *Id.* at §3162.3-1(c); *see* 43 U.S.C. §1732(b).
[88] 43 C.F.R. §3162.3-1(c).
[89] *Id.* at §3162.3-1(d).
[90] *Id.* at §3162.3-1(d), (f).
[91] 30 U.S.C. §226(f); 43 C.F.R. §3162.3-1(g).
[92] 43 C.F.R. §3162.5-1(a).
[93] *Id.*
[94] 43 C.F.R. §3162.3-1(h).
[95] 30 U.S.C. §226(g).
[96] 30 U.S.C. §226(g); 36 C.F.R. §228.106(a).
[97] *Id.*
[98] *Id.*
[99] 30 U.S.C. §228.106(c).
[100] 16 U.S.C. §1604(i); 36 C.F.R. §228.107(a)(2).
[101] 36 C.F.R. §228.107(a).
[102] *Id.* at §228.109(a).
[103] *Id.* at §228.107(b).
[104] *Id.* at §228.107(d).
[105] *Id.* at §203.
[106] 30 U.S.C. §201 *et seq.*
[107] *Id.* at §201(a)(3)(A)(i).
[108] 43 C.F.R. §3420.1-4.

[109] *Id.* at §3420.2.
[110] *Id.* at §§3420.3-3; 3420.3-4.
[111] *Id.* at §3420.3-4(c).
[112] *Id.*
[113] *Id* at §3420.4-2.
[114] *Id.* §§3420.3-3; 3420.4-4.
[115] *Id.* at §3420.5.
[116] *Id.* at §3422.1.
[117] *Id.* at §3422.1(c)
[118] *Id.* at §§3422.3-2; 3422.4
[119] Id. at §§3425.1, 3425.2.
[120] id. at §§3425.1-7; 3425.3.
[121] *Id.* at §3424.4(a)(1).
[122] *Id.* at §3424.4(a)(2).
[123] *Id.* at §3424.4(b).
[124] 30 U.S.C. §184(a).
[125] *Id.* at §201(a)(2).
[126] *Id.* at §207(a).
[127] 43 C.F.R. §3473-3.1(a).
[128] 30 U.S.C. §207(a).
[129] *Id.* at §207(b)(1).
[130] 43 C.F.R. §3474.2.
[131] According to the Geothermal Steam Act, the Secretary of the Interior may issue leases for developments and utilization of geothermal resources in any federal lands administered by BLM, or in national forests administered by the Forest Service, or in lands conveyed by the United States if the conveyance reserved the rights of the United States to the geothermal resources therein. 30 U.S.C. §1002. The act also establishes a number of exceptions to this general leasing authority for certain protected lands. 30 U.S.C. §1014.
[132] *Renewable Energy and the BLM: Geothermal*, fact sheet, available at http://www.blm.gov/pg data/etc/medialib/blm/wo/MINERALS__REALTY__AND_RESOURCE_PROTECTION_/ energy.Par.74240.File.dat/ 09factsheet_Geothermal.pdf.
[133] *Id.*
[134] P.L. 91-581, codified at 30 U.S.C. §§1001 *et seq.*
[135] 43 C.F.R. §3203.10(a). The qualifications for nomination and bidding are set forth at 32 C.F.R. §3202.10.
[136] *Id.* at §3203.10(b).
[137] *Id.* at §3203.11.
[138] *Id.* at §3203.15(b).
[139] *Id.* at §3203.13.
[140] *Id.* at §3203.14 (a)(2).
[141] 30 U.S.C. §1004(a)(3).
[142] 43 C.F.R. §3203.15(c).
[143] *Id.* at §3203.15(b).
[144] *Id.* at §3203.17(b).
[145] *Id.* at §3203.17(c).
[146] *Id.* at §3204.5(a).
[147] *Id.* at §3204.11(a).
[148] *Id.* at §3204.12.
[149] *Id.* at §3205.6(a).
[150] *Id.* at §3207.5.
[151] *Id.* at §3207.11(a).
[152] *Id.* at §3207.12.

[153] *Id.* at §3211.11(b)(1)-(2). For both competitive and non-competitive leases issued before August 8, 2005, the royalty rate is the rate prescribed by regulation as of the date of the issuance of the lease.
[154] *Id.* at §3211.11(b)(3).
[155] *Id.* at §3211.17(a). For earlier leases, the royalty rate varies on a case-by-case basis.
[156] *Id.* at §3211.17(iii).
[157] *Id.* at §3211.18. The applicable fee schedule can be found at 30 C.F.R. 206.356.
[158] 30 U.S.C. §§1010-1011.
[159] *Id.* at §1012.
[160] *Id.* at §1010.
[161] 43 C.F.R. §3251.10. Content requirements for the Notice of Intent are set forth at 43 C.F.R. §3251.11.
[162] *Id.* at §3252.11.
[163] *Id.* at §3253.10.
[164] 43 C.F.R. Subpart 60.
[165] 43 C.F.R. §3262.11.
[166] 43 C.F.R. Subpart 3263.
[167] P.L. 94-579, 43 U.S.C. §§1767 *et seq.*
[168] *Renewable Energy and the BLM: Wind*, January 2009, available at *http://www.blm.gov/* pgdata/etc/medialib/blm/wo/MINERALS__REALTY__AND_RESOURCE_PROTECTIO N_/energy.Par.58306.File.dat/ 09factsheetmap_Wind.pdf.
[169] *Id.*
[170] *Id.*
[171] *Renewable Energy and the BLM: Solar*, July 2009, available at http://www.blm.gov/pgdata/ etc/medialib/blm/wo/MINERALS__REALTY__AND_RESOURCE_PROTECTION_/ener gy.Par.28512.File.dat/09factsheet_Solar.pdf.
[172] *Id.* Areas of Critical Environmental Concern are defined as "those areas within the public lands where special management attention is required ... to protect and prevent irreparable damage to important historical, cultural or scenic values, fish and wildlife resources or other natural systems or processes, or to protect life and safety from natural hazards." 43 U.S.C. §1702(a).
[173] 43 U.S.C. §1761(a)(5).
[174] 43 C.F.R. §2802.10(a).
[175] 43 U.S.C. §1761(b).
[176] *Id.* A detailed review of the information that must in included in an application for a FLPMA right-of-way grant can be found at 43 C.F.R. Subpart 2804.
[177] 43 C.F.R. §2804.14.
[178] *Id.* at §2804.13.
[179] *Id.* at §2805.15(e).
[180] *Id.* at §2805.10(a)(1).
[181] *Id.* at §2805.10(a)(2).
[182] *Id.* at §2805.10(a)(3).
[183] *Id.* at §2806.12.
[184] *Id.* at §2806.15.
[185] *Id.* at §2806.50.
[186] *Id.*
[187] *See* Solar and Wind Energy Applications—Pre-application and Screening, at http://www.blm. gov/wo/st/en/info/regulations/Instruction_Memos_and_Bulletins/national_instruction/2011/ IM_2011-061.html.
[188] *See* Solar and Wind Energy Applications—Due Diligence, available at http://www.blm.gov/ wo/st/en/info/regulations/Instruction_Memos_and_Bulletins/national_instruction/2011/IM_ 2011-060.html.
[189] For more information see BLM's website on the PEIS at http://solareis.anl.gov.

[190] 36 C.F.R. §251.50(a).

[191] The Forest Service Chief is considered the "authorized officer," and the Regional Foresters, Forest Supervisors, District Ranger, or other officer can all serve as "authorized officers" though delegation. 36 C.F.R. §251.52.

[192] 36 C.F.R. §251.52.

[193] *Id.* at §251.53(l)(4).

[194] *Id.* at §251.54(a).

[195] *Id.* at §251.54(e)(1)(i).

[196] *Id.* at §251.54(e)(1)(ii).

[197] *Id.* at §251.54(e)(1)(iv).

[198] *Id.* at §§251.54(e)(1)(iii), (v)-(ix), and (e)(5).

[199] *Id.* at §251.54(g).

[200] *Id.* at §251.54(g)(2)(ii).

[201] *Id.* at §251.54(g)(5).

[202] *Id.* at §251.55(b).

[203] *Id.* at §2151.56.

[204] *Id.* at §251.57(a).

[205] *Id.* at §251.58.

[206] *Id.* at §251.59(a).

[207] *Id.* at §251.56(b).

[208] *Id.* at §251.64(a).

[209] *Id.* at §251.64(b).

In: Energy Projects In Federal Jurisdictions ISBN: 978-1-62100-922-1
Editor: Michael R. Brody

Chapter 2

OFFSHORE OIL AND GAS DEVELOPMENT: LEGAL FRAMEWORK

Adam Vann

SUMMARY

The development of offshore oil, gas, and other mineral resources in the United States is impacted by a number of interrelated legal regimes, including international, federal, and state laws. International law provides a framework for establishing national ownership or control of offshore areas, and domestic federal law mirrors and supplements these standards.

Governance of offshore minerals and regulation of development activities are bifurcated between state and federal law. Generally, states have primary authority in the three-geographical-mile area extending from their coasts. The federal government and its comprehensive regulatory regime govern those minerals located under federal waters, which extend from the states' offshore boundaries out to at least 200 nautical miles from the shore. The basis for most federal regulation is the Outer Continental Shelf Lands Act (OCSLA), which provides a system for offshore oil and gas exploration, leasing, and ultimate development. Regulations run the gamut from health, safety, resource conservation, and environmental standards to requirements for production based royalties and, in some cases, royalty relief and other development incentives.

In 2008, both the President and the 110th Congress removed previously existing moratoria on offshore leasing on many areas of the outer continental shelf. As of the date of this report, Congress has not reinstated the appropriations-based moratoria that were not renewed by the 110th Congress. Other recent legislative and regulatory activity suggests an increased willingness to allow offshore drilling in the U.S. Outer Continental Shelf. In 2006, Congress passed a measure that would allow new offshore drilling in the Gulf of Mexico. Areas of the North Aleutian Basin off the coast of Alaska have also been recently made available for leasing by executive order. The five-year plan for offshore leasing for 2007-2012 adopted by the Minerals Management Service (MMS, now the Bureau of Ocean Energy Management, Regulation, and Enforcement (BOEMRE)) in December of 2007 proposed further expansion of offshore leasing. In the 112th Congress, legislation has been introduced that could accelerate the leasing and permitting process for offshore oil and gas exploration and production. H.R. 1229 would create new deadlines for review of certain permits for exploration and production; while H.R. 1230 would require BOEMRE to lease certain offshore areas for oil and natural gas exploration and production on an accelerated timeline.

In addition to these legislative and regulatory efforts, there has also been significant litigation related to offshore oil and gas development. Cases handed down over a number of years have clarified the extent of the Secretary of the Interior's discretion in deciding how leasing and development are to be conducted.

The development of offshore oil, gas, and other mineral resources in the United States is impacted by a number of interrelated legal regimes, including international, federal, and Tstate laws. International law provides a framework for establishing national ownership or control of offshore areas, and U.S. domestic law has, in substance, adopted these internationally recognized principles. U.S. domestic law further defines U.S. ocean resource jurisdiction and ownership of offshore minerals, dividing regulatory authority and ownership between the states and the federal government based on the resource's proximity to the shore. This report explains the nature of U.S. authority over offshore areas pursuant to international and domestic law. It also describes the laws, at both the state and federal levels, governing the development of offshore oil and gas and the litigation that has flowed from development under these legal regimes. Also included is an outline of recent changes to the authorities regulating offshore development, as well as a discussion of recent executive action and legislative proposals concerning offshore oil and natural gas exploration and production.

OCEAN RESOURCE JURISDICTION

Under the United Nations Convention on the Law of the Sea,[1] coastal nations are entitled to exercise varying levels of authority over a series of adjacent offshore zones. Nations may claim a 12-nautical-mile territorial sea, over which they may exercise rights comparable to, in most significant respects, sovereignty. An additional area, termed the contiguous zone and extending 24 nautical miles from the coast (or baseline), may also be claimed. In this area, coastal nations may regulate, as necessary, to protect the territorial sea and to enforce their customs, fiscal, immigration, and sanitary laws. Further, in the contiguous zone and an additional area, the exclusive economic zone (EEZ), coastal nations have sovereign rights to explore, exploit, conserve, and manage marine resources and assert jurisdiction over:

i. the establishment and use of artificial islands, installations and structures;
ii. marine scientific research; and
iii. the protection and preservation of the marine environment.[2]

The EEZ extends 200 nautical miles from the baseline from which a nation's territorial sea is measured (usually near the coastline). This area overlaps substantially with another offshore area designation, the continental shelf. International law defines a nation's continental shelf as the seabed and subsoil of the submarine areas that extend beyond either "the natural prolongation of [a coastal nation's] land territory to the outer edge of the continental margin, or to a distance of 200 nautical miles from the baselines from which the breadth of the territorial sea is measured where the outer edge of the continental margin does not extend up to that distance."[3] In general, however, under UNCLOS, a nation's continental shelf cannot extend beyond 350 nautical miles from its recognized coastline regardless of submarine geology.[4] In this area, as in the EEZ, a coastal nation may claim "sovereign rights" for the purpose of exploring and exploiting the natural resources of its continental shelf.[5]

Federal Jurisdiction

While a signatory to UNCLOS, the United States has not ratified the treaty. Regardless, many of its provisions are now generally accepted principles of customary international law and, through a series of Executive Orders, the United States has claimed offshore zones that are virtually identical to those described in the treaty.[6] In a series of related cases long before UNCLOS, the U.S. Supreme Court confirmed federal control of these offshore areas.[7] Federal statutes also refer to these areas and, in some instances, define them as well. Of particular relevance, the primary federal law governing offshore oil and gas development indicates that it applies to the "outer Continental Shelf," which it defines as "all submerged lands lying seaward and outside of the areas ... [under state control] and of which the subsoil and seabed appertain to the United States and are subject to its jurisdiction and control...."[8] Thus, the U.S. Outer Continental Shelf (OCS) would appear to comprise an area extending at least 200 nautical miles from the official U.S. coastline and possibly farther where the geological continental shelf extends beyond that point. The federal government's legal authority to provide for and to regulate offshore oil and gas development therefore applies to all areas under U.S. control except where U.S. waters have been placed under the primary jurisdiction of the states.

State Jurisdiction

In accordance with the federal Submerged Lands Act of 1953 (SLA),[9] coastal states are generally entitled to an area extending three geographical miles[10] from their officially recognized coast (or baseline).[11] In order to accommodate the claims of certain states, the SLA provides for an extended three-marine-league[12] seaward boundary in the Gulf of Mexico if a state can show such a boundary was provided for by the state's "constitution or laws prior to or at the time such State became a member of the Union, or if it has been heretofore approved by Congress."[13] After enactment of the SLA, the Supreme Court of the United States held that the Gulf coast boundaries of Florida and Texas do extend to the three-marine-league limit; other Gulf coast states were unsuccessful in their challenges.[14]

Within their offshore boundaries, coastal states have "(1) title to and ownership of the lands beneath navigable waters within the boundaries of the respective states, and (2) the right and power to manage, administer, lease, develop and use the said lands and natural resources...."[15] Accordingly, coastal states have the option of developing offshore oil and gas within their waters; if they choose to develop, they may regulate that development.

Coastal State Regulation

State laws governing oil and gas development in state waters vary significantly from jurisdiction to jurisdiction. Some state laws are limited to a single paragraph and do not differentiate between onshore and offshore state resources; other states do not distinguish between oil and gas and other types of minerals. In addition to regulation aimed specifically at oil and gas development, it should be noted that a variety of other laws could impact offshore development, such as environmental and wildlife protection laws and coastal zone management regulation. Finally, in states that authorize offshore oil and gas leasing, the states decide which offshore areas under their jurisdiction will be opened for development. The Appendix of this report contains a table of state laws regulating and sometimes banning offshore mineral development. The table indicates which state agency is primarily responsible for authorizing oil and gas development and if state oil and gas leasing is limited to specific areas by statute.

FEDERAL RESOURCES

The primary federal law governing development of oil and gas in federal waters is the Outer Continental Shelf Lands Act (OCSLA).[16] As stated above, the OCSLA codifies federal control of the OCS, declaring that the submerged lands seaward of the state's offshore boundaries appertain to the U.S. federal government. More than simply declaring federal control, the OCSLA has as its primary purpose "expeditious and orderly development [of OCS resources], subject to environmental safeguards, in a manner which is consistent with the maintenance of competition and other national needs...."[17] To effectuate this purpose, the OCSLA extends application of federal laws to certain structures and devices located on the OCS;[18] provides that the law of adjacent states will apply to the OCS when it does not conflict with federal law;[19] and, significantly, provides a comprehensive leasing process for certain OCS mineral resources and a system for collecting and distributing royalties from the sale of these federal mineral resources.[20] The OCSLA thus provides comprehensive regulation of the development of OCS oil and gas resources.

Moratoria

In general, the OCSLA requires the federal government to prepare, revise, and maintain an oil and gas leasing program. Until recently, however, many offshore areas were withdrawn from disposition under the OCSLA pursuant to two broad categories of moratoria applicable to OCS oil and gas leasing: those imposed by the President under authority granted by the OCSLA,[21] and those imposed directly by Congress, which have most often taken the form of limitations on the use of appropriated funds.[22]

Appropriations-based congressional moratoria first appeared in the appropriations legislation for FY1982. The language of the appropriations legislation barred the expenditure of funds by the Department of the Interior (DOI) for leasing and related activities in certain areas in the OCS.[23] Similar language appeared in every DOI appropriations bill through FY2008. However, starting with FY2009, Congress has not included this language in appropriations legislation. As a result, the Bureau of Ocean Energy Management, Regulation, and Enforcement (BOEMRE), the agency within the Department of the Interior that administers the OCS exploration and production program, is free to use appropriated funds to fund all leasing, preleasing, and related activities in most OCS areas (where such activities are not prohibited by other legislation).[24] Language used in the legislation that funds DOI in the future will determine whether, and in what form, budget-based restrictions on OCS leasing might return.

In addition to the congressional moratoria, for most of the last 20 years there have been moratoria issued by the executive branch on offshore drilling in many areas. The first of these was issued by President George H. W. Bush on June 26, 1990.[25] This memorandum, issued pursuant to the authority vested in the President under Section 12(a) of the OCSLA, placed under presidential moratoria those areas already under an appropriations-based moratorium pursuant to P.L. 105-83, the Interior Appropriations legislation in place at that time. That appropriations-based moratorium prohibited "leasing and related activities" in the areas off the coast of California, Oregon, and Washington, and the North Atlantic and certain portions of the eastern Gulf of Mexico. The legislation further prohibited leasing, preleasing, and related activities in the North Aleutian basin, other areas of the eastern Gulf of Mexico, and the Mid- and South Atlantic. The presidential moratorium was extended by President Bill Clinton by memorandum dated June 12, 1998.[26]

On July 14, 2008, President George W. Bush issued an executive memorandum that rescinded the executive moratorium on offshore drilling created by the 1990 order of President George H. W. Bush and renewed by President Bill Clinton in 1998.[27] The memorandum revised the language of the previous memorandum so that only areas designated as marine sanctuaries are withdrawn from disposition. The withdrawal has no expiration date.

The July 14, 2008, memorandum, taken together with the expiration of the congressional moratorium, has the effect of opening up areas of the OCS for consideration for exploration and production where such activities had not previously been allowed. OCS acreage not protected by other statutory measures can now be considered by BOEMRE for leasing, as described *infra*. However, it is important to note that other prohibitions and moratoria on development on exploration and production in certain areas of the OCS exist. For example, the Gulf of Mexico Energy Security Act of 2006, enacted as part of H.R. 6111, the Omnibus Tax Relief and Health Care Act of 2006,[28] created a new congressional moratorium over leasing in portions of the OCS that do not depend on annual renewal in appropriations legislation. The 2006 legislation explicitly permits oil and gas leasing in areas of the Gulf of Mexico,[29] but also established a new moratorium on preleasing, leasing, and related activity in the eastern Gulf of Mexico through June 30, 2022.[30] This moratorium is independent of any appropriations-based congressional moratorium, and thus would continue even if Congress reinstated the annual appropriations-based moratorium.

Leasing and Development

In 1978, the OCSLA was significantly amended so as to increase the role of the affected coastal states in the leasing process.[31] The amendments also revised the bidding process and leasing procedures, set stricter criteria to guide the environmental review process, and established new safety and environmental standards to govern drilling operations.

The OCS leasing process consists of four distinct stages: (1) the five-year planning program;[32] (2) preleasing activity and the lease sale;[33] (3) exploration;[34] and (4) development and production.[35] This process has been garnering significant attention in the 112th Congress, where legislation has been introduced that could accelerate the leasing and permitting process for offshore oil and gas exploration and production. H.R. 1229, introduced on March 20, 2011, would create new deadlines for review of certain permits for exploration and production, while H.R. 1230, introduced the same day, would require BOEMRE to lease certain offshore areas for oil and natural gas exploration and production on an accelerated timeline. Given the interest in offshore leasing and permitting in the current Congress, it is worthwhile to explore the details of the process.

The Five-Year Plan

The Secretary of the Interior is required to prepare a five-year leasing plan, subject to annual revisions, that governs any offshore leasing that takes place during the period of plan coverage.[36] Each five-year plan establishes a schedule of proposed lease sales, providing the timing, size, and general location of the leasing activities. This plan is to be based on multiple considerations, including the Secretary's determination as to what will best meet national energy needs for the five-year period and the extent of potential economic, social, and environmental impacts associated with development.[37]

During the development of the plan, the Secretary must solicit and consider comments from the governors of affected states, and at least 60 days prior to publication of the plan in the *Federal Register*, the plan is to be submitted to the governor of each affected state for further comments.[38] After publication, the Attorney General is also authorized to submit comments regarding potential effects on competition.[39] Subsequently, at least 60 days prior to its approval, the plan is to be submitted to Congress and the President, along with any received comments and an explanation for the rejection of any comment.[40] Once the leasing plan is approved, areas included in the plan are to be available for leasing, consistent with the terms of the plan.[41]

The development of the five-year plan is considered a major federal action significantly affecting the quality of the human environment and as such requires preparation of an environmental impact statement (EIS) under the National Environmental Policy Act (NEPA).[42] Thus, the NEPA review process complements and informs the preparation of a five-year plan under the OCSLA.[43]

The current Five-Year Plan took effect on July 1, 2007.[44] The Plan contemplated leasing in areas off the coast of Alaska and in the Central and Western Gulf of Mexico, as well as the possibility of leasing in the mid-Atlantic Ocean Planning Area off the coast of Virginia. In response to calls to expand offshore exploration and production leasing, in July of 2008 MMS took the unprecedented step of initiating a new Five-Year Plan that is expected to commence before the expiration of the previous plan. BOEMRE published notice and a request for comments in the Federal Register regarding a proposed new Five-Year Plan for mid-2010 to mid-2015 that would have replaced the existing Plan.[45] The notice sought "comments on areas that ... were removed from Presidential Withdrawal on July 14, 2008."[46] However, those efforts appear to have stalled. Instead, the current Administration is focusing on expanding offshore exploration and production efforts under the Five-Year Plan that will cover mid-2012 to mid-2017.

The initial scoping evaluation for the 2012-2017 Five-Year Plan included eight different OCS areas, some of which are not currently available for leasing for purposes of oil and natural gas exploration and production.[47] This included areas in the Beaufort Sea, Chukchi Sea, and Cook Inlet in Alaska, the Western, Central and Eastern Gulf of Mexico, and the South Atlantic and Mid-Atlantic Ocean.[48] However, on December 1, 2010, an updated strategy was announced that removed areas in the Eastern Gulf of Mexico and the South Atlantic and Mid-Atlantic Ocean from consideration for leasing under the 2012-2017 Five-Year Plan. The scope of existing leasing activity, as well as areas still under consideration for leasing pursuant to the 2012-2017 Five-Year Plan, is depicted in Figure 1 and Figure 2 below.

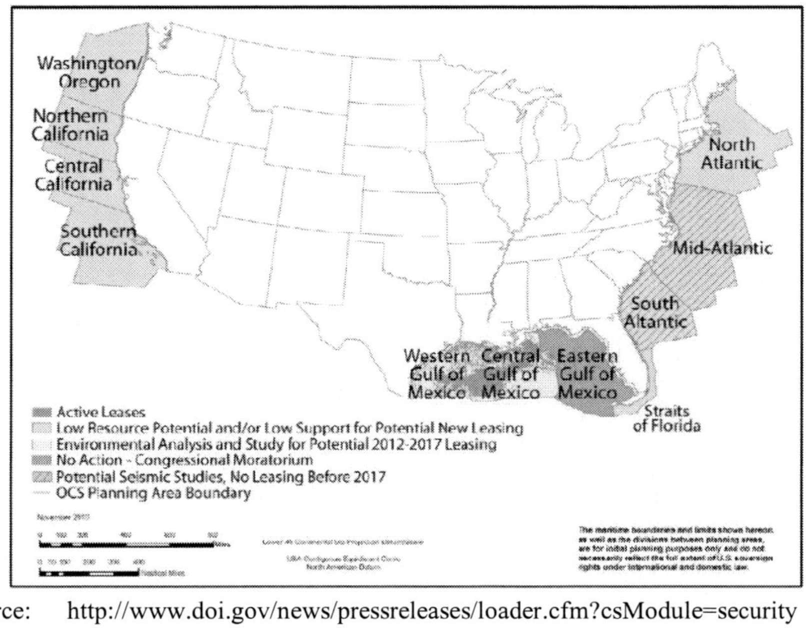

Source: http://www.doi.gov/news/pressreleases/loader.cfm?csModule=security & PageID=78990. Adapted by CRS.

Figure 1. Atlantic, Gulf of Mexico, and Pacific Strategies as of December 1, 2010. Department of the Interior Outer Continental Shelf Oil and Gas Updated Strategy.

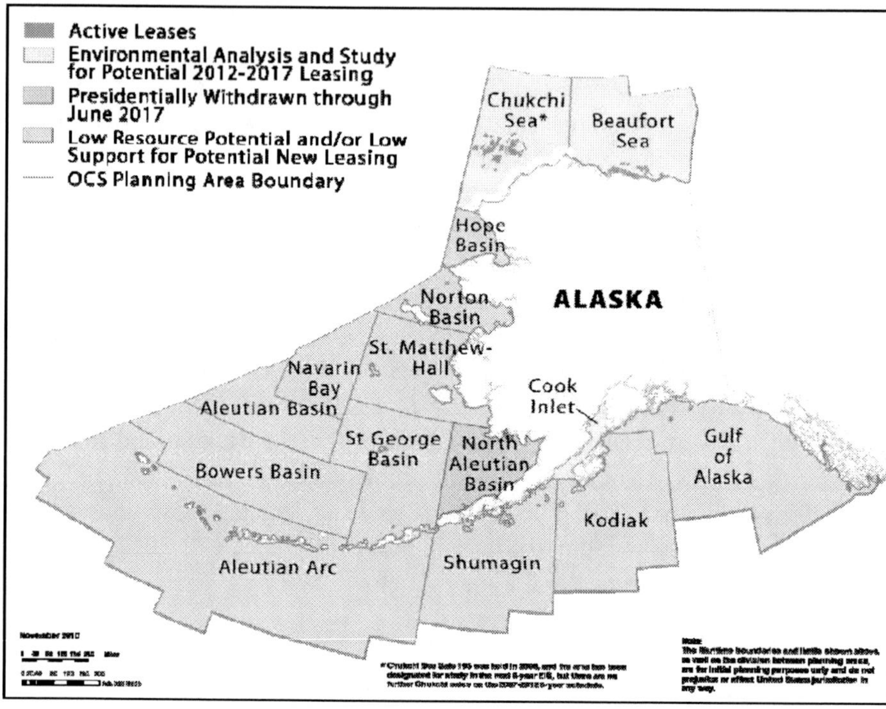

Source: http://www.doi.gov/news/pressreleases/loader.cfm?csModule=security &PageID=78988. Adapted by CRS.

Figure 2. Alaska Strategy as of December 1, 2010.
Department of the Interior Outer Continental Shelf Oil and Gas Updated Strategy.

Leasing

The lease sale process involves multiple steps as well. Leasing decisions are impacted by a variety of federal laws; however, it is section 8 of the OCSLA and its implementing regulations that establish the mechanics of the leasing process.[49]

The process begins when the Director of BOEMRE publishes a call for information and nominations regarding potential lease areas. The Director is authorized to receive and consider these various expressions of interest in lease areas and comments on which areas should receive special concern and analysis.[50] The Director is then to consider all available information and perform environmental analysis under NEPA in crafting both a list of areas recommended for leasing and any proposed lease stipulations.[51] This list is submitted to the Secretary of the Interior and, upon the Secretary's approval, published in the *Federal Register* and submitted to the governors of potentially affected states.[52]

The OCSLA and its regulations authorize the governor of an affected state and the executive of any local government within an affected state to submit to the Secretary any recommendations concerning the size, time, or location[53] of a proposed lease sale within 60 days after notice of the lease sale.[54] The Secretary must accept the governor's recommendations (and has discretion to accept a local government executive's recommendations) if the Secretary determines that the recommendations reasonably balance the national interest and the well-being of the citizens of an affected state.[55]

The Director of BOEMRE publishes the approved list of lease sale offerings in the *Federal Register* (and other publications) at least 30 days prior to the date of the sale.[56] This notice must describe the areas subject to the sale and any stipulations, terms, and conditions of the sale.[57] The bidding is to occur under conditions described in the notice and must be consistent with certain baseline requirements established in the OCSLA.[58]

Although the statute establishes base requirements for the competitive bidding process and sets forth a variety of possible bid formats,[59] some of these requirements are subject to modification at the discretion of the Secretary.[60] Before the acceptance of bids, the Attorney General is also authorized to review proposed lease sales to analyze any potential effects on competition, and may subsequently recommend action to the Secretary of the Interior as may be necessary to prevent violation of antitrust laws.[61] The Secretary is not bound by the Attorney General's recommendation, and likewise, the antitrust review process does not affect private rights of action under antitrust laws or otherwise restrict the powers of the Attorney General or any other federal agency under other law.[62] Assuming compliance with these bidding requirements, the Secretary may grant a lease to the highest bidder, although deviation from this standard may occur under some circumstances.[63]

In addition, the OCSLA prescribes many minimum conditions that all lease instruments must contain. The statute supplies generally applicable minimum royalty or net profit share rates, as necessitated by the bidding format adopted, subject, under certain conditions, to secretarial modification. Several provisions authorize royalty reductions or suspensions. Royalty rates or net profit shares may be reduced below the general minimums or eliminated to promote increased production.[64] For leases located in "the Western and Central Planning Areas of the Gulf of Mexico and the portion of the Eastern Planning Area of the Gulf of Mexico encompassing whole lease blocks lying west of 87 degrees, 30 minutes West longitude and in the Planning Areas offshore Alaska," a broader authority is also provided, allowing the Secretary, with the lessee's consent, to make "other modifications" to royalty or profit share requirements to encourage increased production.[65] Royalties may also be suspended under certain conditions by BOEMRE pursuant to the Outer Continental Shelf Deep Water Royalty Relief Act, discussed *infra*.

The OCSLA generally requires successful bidders to furnish a variety of up-front payments and performance bonds upon being granted a lease.[66] Additional provisions require that leases provide that certain amounts of production be sold to small or independent refiners. Further, leases must contain the conditions stated in the sale notice and provide for suspension or cancellation of the lease in certain circumstances.[67] Finally, the law indicates that a lease entitles the lessee to explore for, develop, and produce oil and gas, conditioned on applicable due diligence requirements and the approval of a development and production plan, discussed below.[68]

Exploration

Exploration for oil and gas pursuant to an OCSLA lease must comply with an approved exploration plan.[69] Detailed information and analysis must accompany the submission of an exploration plan, and, upon receipt of a complete proposed plan, the relevant BOEMRE regional supervisor is required to submit the plan to the governor of an affected state and the state's Coastal Zone Management agency.[70]

Under the Coastal Zone Management Act, federal actions and federally permitted projects, including those in federal waters, must be submitted for state review.[71] The purpose of this review is to ensure consistency with state coastal zone management programs as contemplated by the federal law. When a state determines that a lessee's plan is inconsistent with its coastal zone management program, the lessee must either reform its plan to accommodate those objections and resubmit it for BOEMRE and state approval or succeed in appealing the state's determination to the Secretary of Commerce.[72] Simultaneously, the BOEMRE regional supervisor is to analyze the environmental impacts of the proposed exploration activities under NEPA; however, regulations prescribe that BOEMRE complete its action on the plan review within 30 days. Hence, extensive environmental review at this stage may be constrained or rely heavily upon previously prepared NEPA documents.[73] If the regional supervisor disapproves the proposed exploration plan, the lessee is entitled to a list of necessary modifications and may resubmit the plan to address those issues.[74] Once a plan has been approved, drilling associated with exploration remains subject to the relevant BOEMRE district supervisor's approval of an application for a permit to drill, which involves analysis of even more specific drilling plans.

Development and Production

While exploration often will involve drilling wells, the scale of such activities will significantly increase during the development and production phase. Accordingly, additional regulatory review and environmental analysis are required by the OCSLA before this stage begins.[75] Operators are required to submit a Development and Production Plan for areas where significant development has not occurred before[76] or a less extensive Development Operations Coordination Document for those areas, such as certain portions of the Western Gulf of Mexico, where significant activities have already taken place.[77] The information required to accompany submission of these documents is similar to that required at the exploration phase, but must address the larger scale of operations.[78] As with the processes outlined above, the submission of these documents complements the department's and BOEMRE's environmental analysis under NEPA. It may not always be necessary to prepare a new EIS at this stage, and environmental analysis may be tied to previously prepared NEPA documents.[79] In addition, affected states are allowed, under the OCSLA, to submit comments on proposed Development and Production Plans and to review these plans for consistency with state Coastal Zone Management Programs.[80] Additionally, if the drilling project involves "non-conventional production or completion technology, regardless of water depth," applicants must also submit a Deepwater Operations Plan (DWOP) and a Conceptual Plan.[81] These additional documents allow BOEMRE to review the engineering, safety, and environmental impacts associated with these technologies.[82]

As with the exploration stage, actual drilling requires approval of an Application for Permit to Drill (APD).[83] An APD focuses on the specifics of particular wells and associated machinery. Thus, an application must include a plat indicating the well's proposed location, information regarding the various design elements of the proposed well, and a drilling prognosis, among other things.[84]

Lease Suspension and Cancellation

The OCSLA authorizes the Secretary of the Interior to promulgate regulations on lease suspension and cancellation.[85] The Secretary's discretion over the use of these authorities is specifically limited to a set number of circumstances established by the OCSLA. These circumstances are described below.

Suspension of otherwise authorized OCS activities may generally occur at the request of a lessee or at the direction of the relevant BOEMRE Regional Supervisor, given appropriate justification.[86] Under the statute, a lease may be suspended (1) when it is in the national interest; (2) to facilitate proper development of a lease; (3) to allow for the construction or negotiation for use of transportation facilities; or (4) when there is "a threat of serious, irreparable, or immediate harm or damage to life (including fish and other aquatic life), to property, to any mineral deposits (in areas leased or not leased), or to the marine, coastal, or human environment...."[87] The regulations also indicate that leases may be suspended for other reasons, including (1) when necessary to comply with judicial decrees; (2) to allow for the installation of safety or environmental protection equipment; (3) to carry out NEPA or other environmental review requirements; or (4) to allow for "inordinate delays encountered in obtaining required permits or consents...."[88] Whenever suspension occurs, the OCSLA generally requires that the term of an affected lease or permit be extended by a length of time equal to the period of suspension.[89] This extension requirement does not apply when the suspension results from a lessee's "gross negligence or willful violation of such lease or permit, or of regulations issued with respect to such lease or permit...."[90]

If a suspension period reaches five years,[91] the Secretary may cancel a lease upon holding a hearing and finding that (1) continued activity pursuant to a lease or permit would "probably cause serious harm or damage to life (including fish and other aquatic life), to property, to any mineral (in areas leased or not leased), to the national security or defense, or to the marine, coastal, or human environment"; (2) "the threat of harm or damage will not disappear or decrease to an acceptable extent within a reasonable period of time"; and (3) "the advantages of cancellation outweigh the advantages of continuing such lease or permit in force...."[92]

Upon cancellation, the OCSLA entitles lessees to certain damages. The statute calculates damages at the lesser of (1) the fair value of the canceled rights on the date of cancellation[93] or (2) the excess of the consideration paid for the lease, plus all of the lessee's exploration- or development-related expenditures, plus interest, over the lessee's revenues from the lease.[94]

The OCSLA also indicates that the "continuance in effect" of any lease is subject to a lessee's compliance with the regulations issued pursuant to the OCSLA, and failure to comply with the provisions of the OCSLA, an applicable lease, or the regulations may authorize the Secretary to cancel a lease as well.[95] Under these circumstances, a nonproducing lease can be canceled if the Secretary sends notice by registered mail to the lease owner and the noncompliance with the lease or regulations continues for a period of 30 days after the mailing.[96] Similar noncompliance by the owner of a producing lease can result in cancellation after an appropriate proceeding in any United States district court with jurisdiction as provided for under the OCSLA.[97]

Legal Challenges to Offshore Leasing

Multiple statutes govern aspects of offshore oil and gas development, and therefore, may give rise to legal challenges. Certainly, violations of the Marine Mammal Protection Act,[98] Endangered Species Act,[99] and other environmental laws have provided mechanisms for challenging actions associated with offshore oil and gas production in the past.[100] Of primary interest here, however, are legal challenges to agency action with respect to the planning, leasing, exploration, and development phases under the procedures mandated by the OCSLA itself and the related environmental review required by the National Environmental Policy Act.

Suits under the Outer Continental Shelf Lands Act

The Administrative Procedure Act provides for judicial review of agency action alleged to be in violation of federal law, including the OCSLA, its implementing regulations, and the terms of any permit or lease.[101] The following paragraphs provide an overview of the existing case law and address the limitations applicable to relief at each phase of the leasing and development process.

Jurisdiction to review agency actions taken in approving the five-year plan is vested in the U.S. Court of Appeals for the D.C. Circuit, subject to appellate review by writ of certiorari from the U.S. Supreme Court.[102] A few challenges to five-year plans have been brought. The first, *California ex. rel. Brown v. Watt*,[103] involved a variety of challenges to the 1980-1985 plan, and, while the court ultimately found that the Secretary had failed to comply with certain procedural requirements in making determinations, the court established a relatively deferential standard of review, which it has continued to apply in later challenges. When reviewing "findings of ascertainable fact made by the Secretary," the court will require the Secretary's decisions to be supported by "substantial evidence."[104] However, the court noted that many of the decisions required in the formulation of the five-year plan will involve the determination of policy in the face of disputed facts, and that such determinations should be subject to a less searching standard. In such instances, a court will examine agency action and determine whether "the decision is based on a consideration of the relevant factors and whether there has been a clear error of judgment."[105]

The standards for review outlined in *Watt* have been upheld in subsequent litigation related to the five-year plan.[106] In these subsequent cases, the Court of Appeals for the D.C. Circuit applied a deferential standard in reviewing the Secretary's decisions, particularly in reviewing the Secretary's environmental impact determinations, such that the Secretary could perform environmental analysis using "any methodology so long as it is not irrational."[107] Further, these cases indicate that the Secretary is vested with significant discretion in determining which areas are to be offered for leasing and which areas will not. Thus, while the Secretary must receive and consider comments related to excluding areas from leasing, the court has clearly stated that the Secretary need only identify the legal or factual basis for leasing determinations at this stage and explain those determinations. More searching judicial review of the Secretary's analysis is not required.[108]

Litigation under the OCSLA has also challenged actions taken during the leasing phase. As described above, the OCSLA authorizes states to submit comments during the notice of lease sale stage and directs the Secretary to accept a state's recommendations if they "provide for a reasonable balance between the national interest and the well-being of the citizens of the affected State."[109] Courts have typically applied the deferential "arbitrary and capricious" standard to the Secretary's decisions with respect to these recommendations. According to the cases from the Ninth Circuit Court of Appeals, because the OCSLA does not provide clear guidance as to how balancing of national interest and a state's considerations is to be performed, agency action will generally be upheld so long as "some consideration of the relevant factors ..." takes place.[110] Cases from the federal courts in Massachusetts, including a decision affirmed by the First Circuit Court of Appeals, have, while embracing the arbitrary and capricious standard, found the Secretary's balancing of interests insufficient.[111] However, it should be noted that the Massachusetts cases reviewed agency action that was not supported by explicit analysis of the sort challenged in the Ninth Circuit. Thus, it is possible that, given a more thorough record of the Secretary's decision, these courts may afford more significant deference to the Secretary's determination.

Apart from matters relating primarily to the authority of the Secretary to authorize the various stages of leasing, recent litigation has focused on the authority of MMS/BOEMRE to require royalty payments on certain offshore leases allegedly subject to mandatory royalty relief provisions. In *Kerr-McGee Oil & Gas Corp. v. Allred*, the plaintiff, an oil and gas company operating offshore wells in the Gulf of Mexico pursuant to federal leases, challenged actions by the department to collect royalties on deepwater oil and gas production.[112] The plaintiff alleged the department does not have authority to assess royalties based on an interpretation of the 1995 Outer Continental Shelf Deepwater Royalty Relief Act (DWRRA), that the act requires royalty-free production until a statutorily prescribed threshold volume of oil or gas production has been reached, and does not permit a price-based threshold for this royalty relief.[113]

The DWRRA separates leases into three categories based on date of issuance. These categories are (1) leases in existence on November 28, 1995; (2) leases issued after November 28, 2000; and (3) leases issued in between those periods, that is, during the first five years after the act's enactment. The third category of leases is the source of current controversy. According to Kerr-McGee, its leases, which were issued during the initial five-year period after the DWRRA's enactment, are subject to different legal requirements from those applicable to the other two categories. Kerr-McGee argued that the department has a nondiscretionary duty under the DWRRA to provide royalty relief on its deepwater leases, and that the statute does not provide an exception to this obligation based on any preset price threshold. To the extent any price threshold has been included in these leases, Kerr-McGee argued that such provisions are contrary to DOI's statutory authority and unenforceable.

Section 304 of the DWRRA, which addresses deepwater leases[114] issued within five years after the DWRRA's enactment, directs that such leases use the bidding system authorized in section 8(a)(1)(H) of the OCSLA, as amended by the DWRRA. Section 304 of the DWRRA also stipulates that leases issued during the five-year post-enactment time frame must provide for royalty suspension on the basis of volume. Specifically, section 304 states:

> [A]ny lease sale within five years of the date of enactment of this title, shall use the bidding system authorized in section 8(a)(1)(H) of the Outer Continental Shelf Lands Act, as amended by this title, except that the suspension of royalties shall be set at a volume of not less than the following:

(1) 17.5 million barrels of oil equivalent for leases in water depths of 200 to 400 meters;
(2) 52.5 million barrels of oil equivalent for leases in 400 to 800 meters of water; and
(3) 87.5 million barrels of oil equivalent for leases in water depths greater than 800 meters.[115]

It is possible to interpret this provision as authorizing leases issued during the five-year period to contain *only* royalty suspension provisions that are based on production volume with no allowance at all for a price-related threshold in addition. Such an intent might be gleaned from the language of the quoted section alone; indeed, in this provision, Congress provides for a specific royalty suspension method and does not clearly authorize the Secretary to alter or supplement it. Kerr-McGee's challenge to the Secretary's authority to impose price-based thresholds on royalty suspension was based on this interpretation of the statutory language above.

The U.S. District Court for the Western District of Louisiana agreed with Kerr-McGee's interpretation of the language discussed above. The court found that the DWRRA allowed only for volumetric thresholds on royalty suspension for leases issued between 1996 and 2000, and that the Secretary did not have authority under the DWRRA to attach price-based thresholds to royalty suspension for those leases.[116] On January 12, 2009, the U.S. Court of Appeals for the Fifth Circuit issued a decision affirming the district court's ruling,[117] and on October 5, 2009, the U.S. Supreme Court denied a petition for writ of certiorari.[118]

In *Center for Biological Diversity v. U.S. Department of the Interior*,[119] the plaintiff challenged the five-year plan for 2007-2012 on several grounds. Among these was a claim that DOI had failed to satisfy the requirement found in Section 18(a)(2)(G) of the OCLSA that, in preparing the five-year plan, DOI must consider "the relative environmental sensitivity and marine productivity of different areas of the outer Continental Shelf."[120] The court found that DOI's analysis, which relied solely on "physical characteristics" of different shoreline areas, did not satisfy the requirements of Section 18(a)(2)(G) because it failed to consider non-shoreline areas of the OCS.[121] The court therefore vacated the five-year program and remanded it to DOI for reconsideration. In a later order, the court clarified that this relief related only to those portions of the five-year plan that related to leasing in the Chukchi, Beaufort, and Bering Seas, as the environmental sensitivity analysis for these areas was the only analysis that was found to be deficient.[122]

Suits Under the National Environmental Policy Act

In the context of proposed OCS development, NEPA regulations generally require publication of notice of an intent to prepare an Environmental Impact Statement (EIS), acceptance of comments on what should be addressed in the EIS, agency preparation of a draft EIS, a comment period on the draft EIS, and publication of a final EIS addressing all comments at each stage of the leasing process where government action will significantly affect the environment.[123] As described above, NEPA figures heavily in the OCS planning and leasing process and requires various levels of environmental analysis prior to agency decisions at each phase in the leasing and development process.[124] Lawsuits brought under NEPA are thus indirect challenges to agency decisions in that they typically question the adequacy of the environmental analysis performed prior to a final decision.

In *Natural Resources Defense Council v. Hodel*,[125] the plaintiff challenged the adequacy of the alternatives examined in the EIS and the level of consideration paid to cumulative effects of offshore drilling activities. The court held that not every possible alternative needed to be examined, and that the determination as to adequacy was subject to the "rule of reason."[126] This standard appears to afford some level of deference to the Secretary, and his choice of alternatives was found to be sufficient by the court in this instance.[127] However, without significant explanation of the standard of review to be applied, the court found that the Secretary's failure to analyze certain cumulative impacts was a violation of NEPA.[128] Thus, the Secretary was required to include this analysis, although final decisions based on that analysis remained subject to the Secretary's discretion, with review only under the arbitrary and capricious standard.[129]

As mentioned above, NEPA plays a role in the leasing phase as well. BOEMRE often uses NEPA and its tiering option to evaluate lease sales.[130] The NEPA procedures and standard of review remain the same at this phase; however, due to the structure of the OCSLA process, more specific information is generally required.[131] Still, courts are deferential at the lease sale phase. In challenges to the adequacy of environmental review, courts have stressed that inaccuracies and more stringent NEPA analysis will be available at later phases.[132] Thus, because there will be an opportunity to cure any defects in the analysis as the OCSLA process continues, challenges under NEPA at this phase are often unsuccessful.

It is also possible to challenge exploration and development plans under NEPA. In *Edwardsen v. U.S. Department of the Interior*, the Ninth Circuit Court of Appeals applied the typical "rule of reason" to determine if the EIS adequately addressed the probable environmental consequences of the development and production plan, and held that, despite certain omissions in the analysis and despite an MMS decision to tier its NEPA analysis to an EIS prepared for a similar lease sale, the requirements of NEPA were satisfied.[133] Thus, while additional analysis was required to account for the greater specificity of the plans and to accommodate the "hard look" at environmental impacts NEPA mandates, the reasonableness standard applied to what must be examined in an EIS did not allow for a successful challenge to agency action.

APPENDIX. STATE LAWS THAT BAN OR REGULATE OFFSHORE RESOURCE DEVELOPMENT

Table A-1. State Laws That Ban or Regulate Offshore Resource Development: Policy and Statutes

State	Policy	Statutes
AL	Drilling is authorized in Alabama's state waters. The State Lands Division of the Department of Conservation & Land Resources is charged with leasing offshore oil and gas in state waters. In addition, the Alabama State Oil and Gas Board regulates oil and gas production to ensure the conservation and proper development of oil and gas resources.	**Authorization:** Ala. Code §§ 9-15-18; 9-17-1 *et seq.*; 40-20-1 *et seq.*
AK	The Alaska Department of Natural Resour-ces is responsible for leasing oil and gas on state lands, including offshore areas. Certain areas are specifically designated as off limits to oil and gas leasing, and administrative decisions may further limit access.	**Ban:** Alaska Stat. §§ 38.05.140(f); 38.05.184. **Authorization:** Alaska Stat. §§ 38.05.131 *et seq.*
CA	The State Lands Commission is generally responsible for oil and gas leasing. California currently has a general ban in place restricting any state agency from issuing new offshore leases, unless the President of the United States determines that there is a "severe energy supply interruption and has ordered distribution of the Strategic Petroleum Reserve ... , the Governor finds that the energy resources of the sanctuary will contribute significantly to the alleviation of that interruption, and the Legislature subsequently acts to amend ...[the law] to allow that extraction." The ban is	**Ban:** Cal. Pub. Res. Code §§ 6871.1-.2 (repealed 1994); 6870 (Santa Barbara limitations); 6243 (general ban). **Authorization:** Cal. Pub. Res. Code §§ 6870 *et. seq.*; 6240 *et seq.*

State	Policy	Statutes
	limited to areas that are not currently subject to a lease.	
CT	Connecticut does not appear to have laws addressing oil and gas development in state waters.	
DE	The governor and the secretary of the Department of Natural Resources and Environmental Control are authorized to lease oil and gas in state waters. Lands "administered by the Department of Natural Resources and Environmental Control" may not be leased by the secretary.	**Ban:** Del. Code Ann. tit. 7 ch. 61 § 6102(e). **Authorization:** Del. Code. Ann. tit. 7 ch. 61.
FL	In general, the Department of Natural Resources is vested with the authority to permit oil and gas development on state lands and submerged lands; in 1990, Florida enacted a broad ban on offshore oil and gas development by prohibiting oil and gas drilling structures in a variety of locations, including Florida's territorial waters. The development ban provides an exception for valid existing rights.	**Ban:** Fla. Stat. Ann. § 377.242. **Authorization:** Fla. Stat. Ann. §§ 377.01 *et seq.*; 253.001 *et seq.*
GA	The State Properties Commission is authorized to issue leases for state-owned oil and gas. The statute does not distinguish between onshore and offshore minerals.	**Authorization:** Ga. Stat. § 50-16-43.
HI	The Board of Land and Natural Resources is authorized to lease oil and gas on state lands, including submerged lands. There would not appear to be a statutory ban in place.	**Authorization:** Hawaii Rev. Stat. §§ 182-1 *et seq.*
LA	The state Mineral Board is responsible for leasing oil and gas in Louisiana and its offshore territory. Development is limited to areas offered by the Board for leasing.	**Authorization:** La. Rev. Stat. §§ 30:121 *et seq.*
ME	The Bureau of Geology and Natural Areas has primary authority over oil and gas Development on all state lands. The Bureau is authorized to issue exploration permits and mineral leases.	**Authorization:** Me. Rev. Stat. tit. 12 §§ 549 *et seq.*
MD	The Department of the Environment regulates oil and gas development. The areas underlying the Chesapeake Bay, its tributaries, and the Chesapeake Bay Critical Area are unavailable for oil and gas development.	**Ban:** Md. Code, Envt. § 14-107. **Authorization:** Md. Code, Envt. §§ 14-101 *et seq.*
MA	The Division of Mineral Resources is charged with administering the leasing of oil and gas on state lands. The law requires a public hearing before any	**Authorization:** Mass. Gen. Laws Ann. Ch. 21 §§ 54

Table A-1. (Continued)

State	Policy	Statutes
	license to explore or lease for extraction is issued for mineral resources located in coastal waters. Many of the state's offshore areas are designated as ocean sanctuaries in which oil and gas development is prohibited.	*et seq.* **Ban:** Mass. Gen. Laws Ann. Ch. 132A § 15.
MS	The Mississippi Major Economic Impact Authority is responsible for administering oil and gas leases on state lands. Offshore oil and gas development is generally permissible. Specific areas are not available for leasing. No development may occur in areas north of the coastal barrier islands, except in Blocks 40, 41, 42, 43, 63, 64, and 66 through 98. Further, "surface offshore drilling operations" may not be conducted within one mile of Cat Island.	**Authorization:** Miss. Code. Ann. §§ 29-7-1 *et seq.* **Ban:** Miss. Code. Ann. § 29-7-3.
NH	New Hampshire does not appear to have laws addressing offshore oil and gas development in state waters.	
NJ	State law authorizes the removal of sand and other materials from lands under tidewaters and below the high water mark if approved by the Tidelands Resource Council. Offshore oil and gas development is not addressed.	**Authorization:** N.J. Stat. Ann. §§
NY	Leases and permits for the right to use state- owned submerged lands for navigation, commerce, fishing, bathing, and recreation are authorized for specified sub-merged areas. General authority for issuing oil and gas leases is vested in the Department of Environmental Conservation. Certain submerged lands under-lying specified lakes are excluded from explor-ation and leasing, but offshore areas would not appear to be subject to a similar ban.	**Authorization:** N.Y. Pub. Lands Law § 75; N.Y. Envt'l & Conserv. Law §§ 23- 0101 *et seq.*
NC	State law authorizes the sale or lease of any state-owned mineral underlying the bottoms of any sounds, rivers, creeks, or other waters of the state. The state is authorized to sell, lease, or otherwise dispose of oil and gas at the request of the Department of Environment and Natural Resources.	**Authorization:** N.C. Gen. Stat. § 146-8.
OR	The Department of State Lands is generally responsible for leasing state owned minerals,	**Authorization:** Or. Rev. Stat. §§ 274.705 *et seq.*;

State	Policy	Statutes
	including oil and gas. Leasing of tidal and submerged lands is governed by separate provisions of law. There does not appear to be a ban in place.	273.551 (for submerged lands seaward more than 10 miles easterly of the 124th West Meridian).
RI	The Coastal Resources Management Council is charged with identifying, evaluating, and determining which uses are appropriate for the state's coastal resources and submerged lands.	**Authorization:** R.I. Gen. Laws §§ 46-23-1 *et seq.*
SC	The State Budget and Control Board is authorized to "negotiate for leases of oil, gas and other mineral rights upon all of the lands and waters of the State, including offshore marginal and submerged lands."	**Authorization:** S.C. Code. Ann. §§ 10-9-10 *et seq.*
TX	The School Land Board is authorized to lease those portions of the Gulf of Mexico under the state's jurisdiction for oil and gas development.	**Authorization:** Tex. Nat. Res. Code §§ 52.011 *et seq.*
VA	The Marine Resources Commission is authorized to grant easements or to lease "the beds of the waters of the Commonwealth outside of the Baylor Survey" for oil and gas development.	**Authorization:** Va. Code Ann. § 28.2-1208.
WA	In general, the Department of Natural Resources is responsible for mineral development on state lands. State law prohibits leasing of tidal or submerged lands "extending from mean high tide seaward three miles along the Washington coast from Cape Flattery south to Cape Disappointment, nor in Grays Harbor, Willapa Bay, and the Columbia river downstream from the Longview bridge, for purposes of oil or gas exploration, development, or production."	**Ban:** Wash. Rev. Code Ann. §§ 43.143.005 *et seq.*

Source: CRS.

End Notes

[1] United Nations Convention on the Law of the Sea III (entered into force November 16, 1994) (hereinafter UNCLOS).

[2] *Id.* at Art. 56.1.

[3] *Id.* at Art. 76.1.

[4] *Id.* at Art. 76.4-76.7.

[5] *Id.* at Art. 77.1.

[6] Policy of the United States with Respect to the Natural Resources of the Subsoil and Sea Bed of the Continental Shelf, Proclamation No. 2667, 10 *Fed. Reg.* 12,303 (September 28, 1945);

Exclusive Economic Zone of the United States of America, Proclamation No. 5030, 48 *Fed. Reg.* 10,605 (March 14, 1983); Territorial Sea of the United States of America, Proclamation No. 5928, 54 *Fed. Reg.* 777 (December 27, 1988); Contiguous Zone of the United States, Proclamation No. 7219, 64 *Fed. Reg.* 48,701 (August 2, 1999).

[7] *See* United States v. Texas, 339 U.S. 707 (1950); United States v. Louisiana, 339 U.S. 699 (1950); United States v. California, 332 U.S. 19 (1947). In accordance with the Submerged Lands Act, states generally own an offshore area extending three geographical miles from the shore. Florida (Gulf coast) and Texas, by virtue of their offshore boundaries prior to admission to the Union, have an extended, three-marine-league offshore boundary. *See* United States v. Louisiana, 363 U.S. 1, 36-64 (1960); United States v. Florida, 363 U.S. 121, 121-129 (1960).

[8] 43 U.S.C. § 1331(a).

[9] 43 U.S.C. §§ 1301 *et seq.*

[10] A geographical or nautical mile is equal to 6,080.20 feet, as opposed to a statute mile, which is equal to 5,280 feet.

[11] 43 U.S.C. § 1301(b).

[12] A marine league is equal to 18,228.3 feet.

[13] 43 U.S.C. §§ 1312, 1301(b).

[14] United States v. Louisiana, 363 U.S. 1, 66 (1960) ("[P]ursuant to the Annexation Resolution of 1845, Texas' maritime boundary was established at three leagues from its coast for domestic purposes.... Accordingly, Texas is entitled to a grant of three leagues from her coast under the Submerged Lands Act."); United States v. Florida, 363 U.S. 121, 129 (1960) ("We hold that the Submerged Lands Act grants Florida a three-marine-league belt of land under the Gulf, seaward from its coastline, as described in Florida's 1868 Constitution.").

[15] 43 U.S.C. § 1311.

[16] 43 U.S.C. §§ 1331-1356.

[17] 43 U.S.C. § 1332(3).

[18] 43 U.S.C. § 1333. The provision also expressly makes the Longshore and Harbor Workers' Compensation Act, the National Labor Relations Act, and the Rivers and Harbors Act applicable on the OCS, although application is limited in some instances.

[19] *Id.*

[20] 43 U.S.C. §§ 1331(a), 1332, 1333(a)(1).

[21] 43 U.S.C. § 1341(a).

[22] *See, e.g.*, P.L. 108-447, §§ 107-109.

[23] P.L. 97-100, § 109.

[24] BOEMRE was formerly called the Minerals Management Service. It was renamed pursuant to Secretarial Order 3302, issued on June 18, 2010.

[25] Statement on Outer Continental Shelf Oil and Gas Development, 26 Weekly Comp. Pres. Doc. 1006 (June 26, 1990).

[26] Memorandum on Withdrawal of Certain Areas of the United States Outer Continental Shelf from Leasing Disposition, 34 Weekly Comp. Pres. Doc. 1111 (June 12, 1998).

[27] Memorandum on Modification of the Withdrawal of Certain Areas of the United States Outer Continental Shelf from Leasing Disposition, 44 Weekly Comp. Pres. Doc. 986 (July 14, 2008).

[28] P.L. 109-432.

[29] *Id.* at § 103.

[30] P.L. 109-432, § 104(a).

[31] P.L. 95-372.

[32] 43 U.S.C. § 1344.

[33] 43 U.S.C. §§ 1337, 1345.

[34] 43 U.S.C. § 1340.

[35] 43 U.S.C. § 1351.

[36] 43 U.S.C. § 1344(a), (e).

[37] *Id.*

[38] "Affected state" is defined in the act as any state:

(1) the laws of which are declared, pursuant to section 1333(a)(2) of this title, to be the law of the United States for the portion of the outer Continental Shelf on which such activity is, or is proposed to be, conducted;

(2) which is, or is proposed to be, directly connected by transportation facilities to any artificial island or structure referred to in section 1333(a)(1) of this title;

(3) which is receiving, or in accordance with the proposed activity will receive, oil for processing, refining, or transshipment which was extracted from the outer Continental Shelf and transported directly to such State by means of vessels or by a combination of means including vessels;

(4) which is designated by the Secretary as a State in which there is a substantial probability of significant impact on or damage to the coastal, marine, or human environment, or a State in which there will be significant changes in the social, governmental, or economic infrastructure, resulting from the exploration, development, and production of oil and gas anywhere on the outer Continental Shelf; or

(5) in which the Secretary finds that because of such activity there is, or will be, a significant risk of serious damage, due to factors such as prevailing winds and currents, to the marine or coastal environment in the event of any oil spill, blowout, or release of oil or gas from vessels, pipelines, or other transshipment facilities....

43 U.S.C. § 1331(f).

[39] 43 U.S.C. § 1344(d).

[40] *Id.*; *see also* 30 C.F.R. §§ 256.16-256.17.

[41] 43 U.S.C. § 1344(d).

[42] 42 U.S.C. § 4332(2)(C). In general, NEPA and the regulations that govern its administration require various levels of environmental analysis depending on the circumstances and the type of federal action contemplated. Certain actions that have been determined to have little or no environmental effect are exempted from preparation of NEPA documents entirely and are commonly referred to as "categorical exclusions." In situations where a categorical exclusion does not apply, an intermediate level of review, an environmental assessment (EA), may be required. If, based on the EA, the agency finds that an action will not have a significant effect on the environment, the agency issues a "finding of no significant impact" (FONSI), thus terminating the NEPA review process. On the other hand, major federal actions that are found to significantly affect the environment require the preparation of an environmental impact statement (EIS), a document offering detailed analysis of the project as proposed as well as other options, including taking no action at all. NEPA does not direct an agency to choose any particular course of action; the primary purpose of an EIS is to ensure that environmental consequences are considered. For additional information, see CRS Report RS20621, *Overview of National Environmental Policy Act (NEPA) Requirements*, by Kristina Alexander.

[43] *See* Natural Resources Defense Council v. Hodel, 865 F.2d 288, 310 (D.C. Cir.1988).

[44] The Plan, as revised by Secretary of the Interior Ken Salazar on March 31, 2010, is available on BOEMRE's website at http://www.boemre.gov/5-year/PDFs/PRP2007-2012.pdf.

[45] 73 Fed. Reg. 45065 (August 1, 2008). The notice and request for comment was published by MMS, the predecessor to BOEMRE.

[46] *Id.*

[47] *Notice of Intent to Prepare and Scope an Environmental Impact Statement (EIS) for the Outer Continental Shelf (OCS) Oil and Gas Leasing Program for 2012-2017*, 75 Fed. Reg. 16828 (April 2, 2010).

[48] *Id.*

[49] 43 U.S.C. § 1337.

[50] 30 C.F.R. §§ 256.23, 256.25.

[51] 30 C.F.R. § 256.26.

[52] 30 C.F.R. § 256.29.

[53] It should be noted that the OCSLA establishes certain minimum requirements applicable to these subjects. For instance, lease tracts are, in general, to be limited to 5,760 acres, unless the Secretary determines that a larger area is necessary to comprise a "reasonable economic production unit...." *Id.* at § 1337(b). The law and its implementing regulations also set the range of initial lease terms and baseline conditions for lease renewal.

[54] 43 U.S.C. § 1345(a); *see also* 30 C.F.R. § 256.31.

[55] 43 U.S.C. § 1345(c).

[56] 43 U.S.C. § 1337(*l*).

[57] 30 C.F.R. § 256.32(1).

[58] 43 U.S.C. § 1337.

[59] 43 U.S.C. § 1337(a)(1)(A)-(H). For example, bids may be on the basis of "cash bonus bid with a royalty at not less than 12 ½ per centum fixed by the Secretary in amount or value of the production saved, removed, or sold...." *See also* 30 C.F.R. §§ 256.35-256.47.

[60] 43 U.S.C. §§ 1337(a)(1)-(3), (8)-(9).

[61] 43 U.S.C. § 1337(c); 30 C.F.R. § 256.47(d).

[62] 43 U.S.C. § 1337(c), (f).

[63] Restrictions include a statutory prohibition on issuance of a new lease to a bidder that is not meeting applicable due diligence requirements with respect to the bidder's other leases. *See* 43 U.S.C. § 1337(d).

[64] *Id.* at § 1337(a)(3).

[65] 43 U.S.C. § 1337(a)(3)(B).

[66] 43 U.S.C. § 1337(a)(7); 30 C.F.R. §§ 256.52-256.59.

[67] 43 U.S.C. § 1337.

[68] 43 U.S.C. § 1337(b)(4).

[69] 43 U.S.C. § 1340(b), (c).

[70] 30 C.F.R. §§ 250.226, 250.227, 250.232, 250.235.

[71] 16 U.S.C. § 1456(c).

[72] 30 C.F.R. § 250.235.

[73] 30 C.F.R. § 250.232(c).

[74] 30 C.F.R. §§ 250.231-250.233.

[75] 43 U.S.C. § 1351.

[76] 30 C.F.R. § 250.201.

[77] *Id.*

[78] 30 C.F.R. §§ 250.24-250.262.

[79] The regulations indicate that "at least once in each planning area (other than the western and central Gulf of Mexico planning areas) we [BOEMRE] will prepare an environmental impact statement (EIS)...." 30 C.F.R. § 250.269.

[80] 30 C.F.R. § 250.267.

[81] 30 C.F.R. §§ 250.286, 250.287.

[82] 30 C.F.R. §§ 250.289, 250.292.

[83] 30 C.F.R. §§ 250.410-250.469.

[84] 30 C.F.R. § 250.411.

[85] 43 U.S.C. § 1334; *see also* 30 C.F.R. §§ 250.168-250.185.

[86] 30 C.F.R. §§ 250.168, 250.171-250.175.

[87] 43 U.S.C. § 1334(a)(1).

[88] 30 C.F.R. § 250.173-250.175.

[89] 43 U.S.C. § 1334(a)(1).

[90] *Id.*

[91] 43 U.S.C. § 1334(a)(2)(B). The requisite suspension period may be reduced upon the request of the lessee.

[92] 43 U.S.C. § 1334(a)(2)(A)(i)-(iii). For regulations implementing the cancellation provisions, see 30 C.F.R. §§ 250.180-250.185.

[93] The statute requires "fair value" to take account of "anticipated revenues from the lease and anticipated costs, including costs of compliance with all applicable regulations and operating orders, liability for cleanup costs or damages, or both, in the case of an oil spill, and all other costs reasonably anticipated on the lease...." 43 U.S.C. § 1334(a)(2)(C).

[94] Exceptions from this method of calculation are carved out for leases issued before September 18, 1978, and for joint leases that are canceled due to the failure of one or more partners to exercise due diligence. 43 U.S.C. § 1334(a)(2)(C)(ii)(I), (II); *see also* 30 C.F.R. §§ 250.184-250.185.

[95] 43 U.S.C. § 1334(b).

[96] 43 U.S.C. § 1334(c).

[97] 43 U.S.C. § 1334(d).

[98] 16 U.S.C. §§ 1361-1423.

[99] 16 U.S.C. §§ 1531-1544.

[100] Village of Akutan v. Hodel, 869 F.2d 1185 (9th Cir. 1988); Village of False Pass v. Clark, 733 F.2d 605 (9th Cir. 1984); North Slope Borough v. Andrus, 642 F.2d 589 (D.C. Cir. 1980); Conservation Law Foundation v. Andrus, 623 F.2d 712 (1st Cir. 1979).

[101] 43 U.S.C. § 1349.

[102] 43 U.S.C. § 1349(c).

[103] 668 F.2d 1290 (D.C. Cir. 1981).

[104] *Id.* at 1302; *see also* 43 U.S.C. § 1349(c)(6).

[105] *Id.* at 1301-1302 (*quoting* Citizens to Preserve Overton Park v. Volpe, 401 U.S. 402, 416 (1971) (internal quotations omitted)).

[106] *See* California v. Watt, 712 F.2d 584 (D.C. Cir. 1983); Natural Resources Defense Council v. Hodel, 865 F.2d 288 (D.C. Cir. 1988).

[107] *California*, 712 F.2d at 596 (internal quotations omitted).

[108] *Hodel*, 865 F.2d at 305.

[109] 43 U.S.C. § 1345(d).

[110] California v. Watt, 683 F.2d 1253, 1269 (9th Cir. 1982); *see also* Tribal Village of Akutan v. Hodel, 869 F.2d 1185 (9th Cir. 1988).

[111] Conservation Law Foundation v. Watt, 560 F.Supp. 561 (D.Mass. 1983), aff'd sub nom. Massachusetts v. Watt, 716 F.2d 946 (1st Cir. 1983); Massachusetts v. Clark, 594 F.Supp. 1373 (D.Mass. 1984).

[112] Kerr-McGee v. Allred, No, 2:06 CV 0439, 2007 WL 3231634 (W.D. La. Oct. 30, 2007).

[113] P.L. 104-58.

[114] This term refers to "tracts located in water depths of 200 meters or greater in the Western and Central Planning Area of the Gulf of Mexico, including that portion of the Eastern Planning Area of the Gulf of Mexico encompassing whole lease blocks lying west of 87 degrees, 30 minutes West longitude...." 43 U.S.C. § 1337 note.

[115] P.L. 104-58.

[116] Kerr-McGee v. Allred, slip. op. at 8-9.

[117] Kerr-McGee Oil & Gas Corp. v. U.S. Dep't of Interior, 554 F.3d 1082 (5th Cir. 2009).

[118] U.S. Dept. of the Interior v. Kerr-McGee Oil and Gas Corp., 130 S. Ct. 236 (Mem) (2009).

[119] 563 F.3d 466 (D.C. Cir. 2009).

[120] 43 U.S.C. § 1344(a)(2)(G).

[121] 563 F.3d at 488.

[122] Center for Biological Diversity v. U.S. Department of the Interior; Order upon consideration of respondent's petition for rehearing and/or clarification, No. 07-1247 (D.C. Cir. July 28, 2009).

[123] 40 C.F.R. §§ 1501.7, 1503.1, 1503.4, 1506.10.

[124] 42 U.S.C. § 4332.

[125] 865 F.2d 288 (D.C. Cir. 1988).

[126] *Id.* at 294.

[127] *Id.* at 296.

[128] *Id.* at 297-300.

[129] *See* California ex. rel. Brown v. Watt, 668 F.2d 1290, 1301-1302 (D.C. Cir. 1981).

[130] *See* 30 C.F.R. § 256.26(b); 40 C.F.R. § 1508.28.

[131] Tribal Village of Akutan v. Hodel, 869 F.2d 1185, 1191 (9th Cir. 1988).

[132] *Id.* at 1192; Alaska v. Andrus, 580 F.2d 465, 473 (D.C. Cir. 1978); Village of False Pass v. Clark, 733 F.2d 605, 612-616 (9th Cir. 1984); North Slope Borough v. Andrus, 642 F.2d 589, 594-905 (D.C. Cir. 1980).

[133] 268 F.3d 781, 784-790 (9th Cir. 2001).

In: Energy Projects In Federal Jurisdictions ISBN: 978-1-62100-922-1
Editor: Michael R. Brody

Chapter 3

WIND ENERGY: OFFSHORE PERMITTING

Adam Vann

SUMMARY

Technological advancement, financial incentives, and policy concerns have driven a global expansion in the development of renewable energy resources. Wind energy, in particular, is now often cited as the fastest-growing commercial energy source in the world. Currently, all U.S. wind energy facilities are based on land. However, multiple offshore projects have been proposed and are at various stages of the federal permitting process.

The United States has the authority to permit and regulate offshore wind energy development within the zones of the oceans under its jurisdiction. The federal government and coastal states each have roles in the permitting process, the extents of which depend on whether the project is located in state or federal waters. Currently, no single federal agency has exclusive responsibility for permitting related to activities on submerged lands in federal waters; authority is allocated among various agencies based on the nature of the resource to be exploited and the potential impacts incidental to such exploitation. The same is true for the offshore wind energy context, where several federal agencies have a role to play in permitting development and operation activities.

Section 388 of the Energy Policy Act of 2005 (EPAct; P.L. 109-58) amended the Outer Continental Shelf Lands Act (OCSLA) to address previous uncertainties regarding offshore wind projects. This provision retained a role for the Army Corps of Engineers in permitting under the Rivers and Harbors Act but grants ultimate authority over offshore wind energy development to the Secretary of the Interior. The provision also contained various exemptions from the regulatory regime it establishes for projects that received certain permits prior to the enactment of EPAct. The statutory authority granted by section 388 is administered by the Bureau of Ocean Energy Management, Regulation, and Enforcement (BOEMRE), an agency within the Department of the Interior (DOI).

Technological advancements and tax incentives have driven a global expansion in the development of renewable energy resources. Wind energy, in particular, is now often cited as the fastest-growing commercial energy source in the world;[1] and U.S. wind energy production capacity has been increasing consistently over the past several years.[2] Currently, unlike much of Europe,[3] all wind power facilities in the United States are based on land. However, multiple offshore projects have been proposed in recent years, including the Cape Wind project off the coast of Massachusetts; Deepwater Wind's proposals off the coasts of Massachusetts, Rhode Island, New York, and New Jersey; and a Galveston-Offshore Wind, LLC project in a portion of the Gulf of Mexico under the jurisdiction of Texas.[4]

The focus of this report is the current law applicable to siting offshore wind facilities, including the relationship between state and federal jurisdictional authorities.[5] This report also discusses the court challenges to early federal offshore wind energy permitting authorities and the effect that the Energy Policy Act of 2005[6] has had on the regulatory environment.

JURISDICTION OVER THE OCEAN

As a primary matter, it is important to briefly review the source of federal and state claims of jurisdiction over the Outer Continental Shelf

United States authority in the oceans begins at the coast—called the baseline—and extends 200 nautical miles out to sea. The first 12 nautical miles comprise the U.S. territorial sea.[7] Under the 1982 United Nations Convention on the Law of the Sea[8] (UNCLOS), a coastal nation may claim sovereignty over the air space, water, seabed, and subsoil within its territorial sea.[9] U.S. Supreme Court precedent and international practice indicate that this sovereignty authorizes coastal nations to permit offshore development within their territorial seas.[10] Although the United States has not ratified UNCLOS, it generally acts in alignment with its terms.

The U.S. contiguous zone extends beyond the territorial sea to 24 nautical miles from the baseline. In this area, a coastal nation may regulate to protect its territorial sea and to enforce its customs, fiscal, immigration, and sanitary laws[11]

The relative jurisdiction of the federal government with respect to individual states is also of importance. The Submerged Lands Act of 1953[12] assured coastal states title to the lands beneath coastal waters in an area stretching, in general, three geographical miles from the shore.[13] Thus, states may regulate the coastal waters within this area, subject to federal regulation for "commerce, navigation, national defense, and international affairs" and the power of the federal government to preempt state law.[14] The remaining outer portions of waters over which the United States exercises jurisdiction are federal waters.[15]

It would seem relatively clear that the federal government would have permitting authority for offshore wind farms, to the outer boundaries of its Exclusive Economic Zone (EEZ). However, federal authority would be limited by the internationally recognized right of free passage and by the jurisdiction granted to the states under the Submerged Lands Act. The scope of this federal authority is discussed in greater detail later in this report.

State Permitting

States play an important regulatory role when a wind energy project is proposed for construction in federal or state waters. Under the Coastal Zone Management Act[16] (CZMA) states are encouraged to enact coastal zone management plans to coordinate protection of habitats and resources in coastal waters.[17] The CZMA establishes a policy of preservation alongside sustainable use and development compatible with resource protection.[18] State coastal zone management programs that are approved by the Secretary of Commerce receive federal monetary and technical assistance. State programs must designate conservation measures and permissible uses for land and water resources[19] and must address various sources of water pollution.[20]

The CZMA also requires that the federal government and federally permitted activities comply with state programs.[21] Responding to a Supreme Court decision that excluded oil and gas leasing in the federal waters of the Outer Continental Shelf (OCS) from state review under the CZMA, Congress amended the "consistency review" provision to include the impacts on a state coastal zone from actions in federal waters.[22] Thus, states have some authority to seek consistency between federal efforts to permit projects in federal waters and state coastal zone management regulation.

In addition to consistency review, projects to be constructed in state waters, including any cables that would be necessary to transmit power back to shore, are subject to all state regulation or permitting requirements. Coastal zone regulation varies significantly among the states. The CZMA itself establishes three generally acceptable regulatory frameworks: (1) "State establishment of criteria and standards for local implementation, subject to administrative review and enforcement;" (2) "[d]irect State land and water use planning and regulation;" and (3) regulation development and implementation by local agencies, with state-level review of program decisions.[23]

Within these frameworks, several states, such as New Jersey, California, and Rhode Island, consolidate authority for their programs in one agency.[24] In New Jersey, for instance, the state Department of Environmental Protection (through the Coastal Management Office within the Commissioner's Office of Policy, Planning, and Science) is the lead agency for coastal zone management under several state laws.[25] The majority of states, however, operate coastal zone management programs under "networks" of parallel agencies, with various roles defined by policy guidance and memoranda of understanding (MOUs).[26] Based on a series of MOUs, each agency is obligated to issue and apply state regulations and permits consistently with the state's coastal zone management program.[27] Thus, offshore wind energy projects could be subject to comprehensive regulation with permitting authority spread among multiple state and local agencies.

FEDERAL PERMITTING

Use of federal and federally controlled lands, including the OCS, requires some form of permission, such as a right-of-way, easement, or license.[28] For *onshore* wind projects on federal public lands, the Department of the Interior (DOI), through the Bureau of Land Management, has created a regulatory program under the Federal Land Policy and Management Act,[29] but a federal statute expressly governing *offshore* wind energy development was not enacted until August 2005 as part of the Energy Policy Act of 2005 (EPAct). Before enactment of EPAct, some permitting in support of offshore wind energy development had taken place under laws existing at that time. Use of these authorities proved controversial and was the subject of a lawsuit challenging preliminary permitting actions. The previous regulatory regime, the conflicts it engendered, and EPAct legal authority are discussed below.

The Energy Policy Act of 2005

Prior to enactment of EPAct, the Army Corp of Engineers (Corps) took the lead role in the federal offshore wind energy permitting process, claiming jurisdiction pursuant to section 10 of the Rivers and Harbors Act (RHA),[30] as amended by the Outer Continental Shelf Lands Act (OCSLA).[31] The Corps has jurisdiction under these laws to permit obstructions to navigation within the "navigable waters of the United States" and on the OCS.[32] The Corps' jurisdiction over potential offshore wind projects had never been made explicit, however.

Section 388 of EPAct seeks to address some of the uncertainty related to federal jurisdiction over offshore wind energy development by amending the OCSLA to specifically establish legal authority for federal review and approval of various offshore energy-related projects. The provision amended the OCSLA by adding a new subsection that authorizes the Secretary of the Interior, in consultation with other federal agencies, to grant leases, easements, or rights-of-way on the OCS for certain activities—wind energy development among them—not authorized by other OCSLA provisions, the Deepwater Port Act, the Ocean Thermal Energy Conversion Act, or "other applicable law."[33] A memorandum of understanding between the Department of the Interior and the Federal Energy Regulatory Commission (FERC) signed in April of 2009 confirmed the exclusive jurisdiction of the Secretary of the Interior, exercised through the Bureau of Ocean Energy Management, Regulation and Enforcement (BOEMRE),[34] an agency within DOI, over "the production, transportation, or transmission of energy from non-hydrokinetic renewable energy projects on the OCS."

EPAct also makes clear that federal agencies with permitting authority under other federal laws retain their jurisdiction, despite enactment of this subsection.[35] Thus, the Corps continues to permit offshore development pursuant to the RHA, and other federal agencies with jurisdiction over issues related to energy development, such as species impacts, are similarly unaffected.

The act does not clarify which agency should take the lead role in coordinating federal permitting and responsibility for preparing analysis under the National Environmental Policy Act (NEPA).[36] However, several provisions within section 388 indicate that DOI is charged with primary responsibility. The law directs the Secretary of the Interior to consult with other agencies as a part of its leasing, easement, and right-of way granting process.[37] DOI is also responsible for ensuring that activities carried out pursuant to its new authority provide for "coordination with relevant federal agencies."[38] The law also directs the Secretary to establish a system of "royalties, fees, rentals, bonuses, or other payments" that will ensure a fair return to the United States for any property interest granted under this provision.[39]

Although section 388 of EPAct provides DOI with significant flexibility in crafting a regulatory regime for offshore wind energy development, the act did address certain aspects of the property interest granting process. First, the act directed that leases, easements, and rights-of-way are to be issued on a competitive basis, subject to some exceptions as described *infra.*[40] The Secretary is further authorized to provide for the duration of any property interest granted under this subsection and to provide for suspension and cancellation of any lease, easement, or right-of-way.[41]

Section 388 of EPAct also establishes the method for allocation among states of royalty and other payments collected by the government pursuant to offshore permitting. The allocation is to be based upon a formula that equitably distributes 27% of the revenues collected by the government, based on the proximity of the project to the affected states' offshore boundaries. [42] The act established that states that have a "coastline that is located within 15 miles of the geographic center of the project" are entitled to a revenue share.[43] More than one state may be eligible to receive a portion of these revenues, depending upon the location of a project.

In addition, EPAct appears to authorize considerable regulation of impacts associated with offshore development by requiring the Secretary to ensure that "any activity under this subsection" be carried out in a manner that adequately addresses specified issues, including environmental protection, safety, protection of U.S. national security, and protection of the rights of others to use the OCS and its resources.[44] This subsection also establishes specific financial security requirements for projects. The law requires the holder of a section 388 property interest to "provide for the restoration of the lease, easement, or right-of-way" and to furnish a surety bond or other form of security, leaving the amount and the exact purposes to which any forfeited sums will be applied to the Secretary's discretion.[45] Further, in conjunction with the authority to require some form of financial assurance, the Secretary is empowered to impose "such other requirements as the Secretary considers necessary to protect the interests of the public and the United States."[46] Thus, the Secretary, depending on how these authorities are exercised, may potentially regulate many aspects of any industry that is permitted to operate on the OCS under this subsection of the OCSLA.

EPAct also contains a provision expressly providing for a state consultative role in the permitting process. Section 388 requires the Secretary of the Interior to provide for coordination and consultation with a state's governor or the executive of any local government that may be affected by a lease, easement, or right-of-way granted under this new authority.[47] In addition, the law makes clear that it does not affect any state's claim to "jurisdiction over, or any right, title, or interest in, any submerged lands."[48]

On April 29, 2009, the Minerals Management Service (MMS) issued a fmal rule establishing the permitting process and setting forth a royalty collection and allocation structure for OCS energy projects, as directed by EPAct.[49] The rulemaking created a system whereby BOEMRE[50] will issue two types of OCS leases. Limited leases would grant access and operational rights to the lessee for activities related to the production of energy, including assessment and testing activities, but would not authorize production of energy products for sale or distribution.[51] Commercial leases would give the lessee full rights to receive authorizations necessary to assess, test, and produce renewable energy on a commercial scale over the long term (approximately 30 years).[52]

The rulemaking sets forth a formula for determining payment amounts, including lease payments and royalties, owed by parties participating in OCS renewable energy projects.[53] The rulemaking also establishes the method of allocation of the revenues received by the federal government from these parties. As mandated by EPAct, BOEMRE shares 27% of these revenues with affected states. The rulemaking explains that if any area of a project is within three miles of any state submerged lands, the federal revenues from that project will be shared with the states.[54] Revenues from such projects are to be shared with all states within 15 miles of the geographical center of the project.[55] Revenues from a project will not be shared with a state if the nearest point on its coastline is more than 15 miles from the geographic center of a qualified project area, even if a portion of the qualified project area is located within 3 nautical miles of that state's seaward boundary.[56] The proportionate revenue sharing will be based on the objective measure of the lease area active at the end of the fiscal year in which BOEMRE collects the sharable revenue.[57] The configuration of the area on the last day of the fiscal year is used to determine eligible state payments for that year.[58]

EPAct Exemptions

As described above, section 388 of EPAct expands federal OCS leasing law to include wind energy production and sets forth procedures for granting a lease, easement, or right-of-way in federal waters.[59] However, subsection (d) exempts certain actions from specific section 388 requirements. This "savings provision" states that the law does not require

> the resubmittal of any document that was previously submitted or the reauthorization of any action that was previously authorized with respect to a project for which, before the date of enactment of this Act-
> (1)an offshore test facility has been constructed; or
> (2)a request for a proposal has been issued by a public authority.

Thus, where a project has resulted from a public entity's request for proposals or where a project is associated with an existing offshore test facility, previously submitted documents do not need to be resubmitted and previously authorized actions do not need to be reauthorized, essentially maintaining the status quo with respect to these projects.[60] This provision does not seem to exempt *unauthorized* actions associated with the exempted actions, or, indeed, any other aspect of the related project, from a requirement to comply with the property interest acquisition provisions of section 388. Thus, siting and construction of an offshore data tower, such as Cape Wind's data tower in Nantucket Sound, would not have to be reauthorized. However, any activity that had not been authorized before EPAct's enactment on August 8, 2005, such as the construction of additional facilities, would appear to be subject to the requirements of section 388.

Section 388 also contains two exceptions to the general requirement that a property interest issued under this provision be granted on a "competitive basis": (1) if the Secretary of the Interior determines that there is no competitive interest, or (2) if the project meets the criteria established by the savings provision in subsection (d).[61] The first exemption, requiring a fmding of no competitive interest, is relatively straightforward, and applies if there are not multiple parties interested in a particular property interest. The second exemption, however, is more complex in that it may apply more broadly than the savings provision itself As the text of the statute indicates, "projects that meet the criteria established under section 388(d)" are exempted from the requirement of competitive property interest acquisition.[62] It is not clear that the *projects* referenced are limited to the actions (such as a data tower constructed at the time of EPAct's enactment) previously authorized. Subsection (d) appears to use the term *project* more broadly, such that a "project for which ... an offshore test facility has been constructed" might encompass all future offshore development that would be supported by, or is in some way related to, a qualifying test facility.[63] It is also possible that a *project* for which a test facility has been constructed could be interpreted more narrowly, such that the term *project* would include only those actions authorized in conjunction with the test facility itself In short, because there is no definition provided for *project* in the applicable statute, it would seem likely that the administering agency would be responsible for providing a definition that is reasonably supportable by the statute.

Legal and Regulatory Developments Since EPAct

As described above, EPAct intended to set forth a clearer new regulatory scheme for permitting and regulation of offshore wind energy projects. MMS's 2009 fmal rule provides further details about the leasing process and the collection and allocation of prospective royalties associated with the permitting of offshore wind facilities. However, MMS/BOEMRE has continued working to clarify any potential ambiguities or hurdles to the offshore wind leasing and permitting process. In late 2009 and early 2010, MMS set up "Task Forces" with officials from a number of coastal states and has held initial meetings with many of these Task Forces.[64] According to MMS, these Task Forces were intended to "provide a forum for efficient review of proposed renewable energy projects on the OCS to move toward the goal of expanding our nation's energy resource portfolio in an environmentally sound manner, while being responsive to the needs of affected States, localities and tribes."[65] The use of these Task Forces was established in the April 2009 Final Rule on renewable energy development in the OCS discussed above.

MMS/BOEMRE has also continued to work to resolve other potential legal hurdles in OCS wind energy development through memoranda of understanding (MOUs) with other federal agencies. As discussed above, in April of 2009 MMS and FERC agreed to an MOU regarding regulatory jurisdiction over offshore renewable energy projects. In addition, in June of 2009 MMS and the U.S. Fish and Wildlife Service (FWS) entered into an MOU regarding the protection of Migratory Birds pursuant to the requirements of the Migratory Bird Treaty Act and the executive order directing its implementation.[66] In the MOU, MMS committed to "[p]rotect, restore and enhance habitat of migratory birds to the extent practicable during the MMS's management of resource development and extraction."[67]

Additional Laws and Regulations of Note

In addition to the regulatory regime authorized by section 388, it is also noteworthy that a variety of laws predating the enactment of EPAct remain applicable to offshore wind energy development. The act makes clear that section 388 does not affect the jurisdiction, responsibility, or authority of any federal or state agency operating under other federal law.[68] Thus, it would seem that the state role provided for by the CZMA and the Corps permitting authority provided by the RHA, both described above, remain intact. Other federal laws that are likely to be relevant in the permitting process are described below.

First, the Department of the Interior and any cooperating federal, state, or local entities are required to undertake an environmental review process mandated by the National Environmental Policy Act (NEPA).[69] NEPA requires federal agencies to take a "hard look" at, and to disclose, the environmental consequences of their actions. In general, NEPA and its implementing regulations require various levels of environmental analysis depending on the circumstances and the type of federal action contemplated. Certain actions that have been determined to have little or no environmental effect are exempted from preparation of NEPA documents entirely and are commonly referred to as "categorical exclusions."[70] In situations where a categorical exclusion does not apply, an intermediate level of review, an environmental assessment (EA), may be required. If, on the basis of the EA, the agency fords that an action will not have a significant effect on the environment, the agency issues a "fmding of no significant impact" (FONSI), thus terminating the NEPA review process. On the other hand, major federal actions that are found to significantly affect the environment require the preparation of an environmental impact statement (EIS), a document containing detailed analysis of the project as proposed, as well as other options, including taking no action at all. NEPA does not direct an agency to choose any particular course of action; the only purpose of an EIS is to ensure that environmental consequences are considered. Thus, in practice, NEPA review will likely provide information on wind energy projects, including impacts on

> existing resources of the final alternative sites in terms of physical oceanography and geology; wildlife, avian, shellfish, finfish and benthic habitat; aesthetics, cultural resources, socioeconomic conditions, and air and water quality. Human uses such as boating and fishing will also be described.[71]

In addition to the role interested parties and cooperating agencies may play under NEPA, certain federal agencies have independent sources of jurisdiction over specific ocean resources. Thus, they would also likely be involved in the permitting of offshore wind energy facilities. Some of the most relevant authorities are the Endangered Species Act (ESA),[72] the Marine Mammal Protection Act (MMPA),[73] and the Migratory Bird Treaty Act (MBTA).[74]

Briefly, each of these laws sets parameters for federal activities that potentially inflict certain kinds of harm upon designated species of plants and animals. The ESA prohibits any person, including private entities, from "taking" a "listed" species.[75] *Take* is broadly defined as "to harass, harm, pursue, hunt, shoot, wound, kill, trap, capture or collect, or to attempt to engage in any such conduct."[76] Additionally, a federal agency permitting or undertaking action that could impact a protected species is subject to section 7 of the ESA, which requires consultation with the U.S. Fish and Wildlife Service (FWS) or the National Marine Fisheries Service (NMFS or NOAA Fisheries), depending upon the species affected.[77]

The section 7 consultation process involves several initial steps leading to a determination of whether a listed species or its designated critical habitat is present in a project area.[78] If a listed species or critical habitat is present, then the permitting/acting federal agency must prepare a biological assessment, evaluating the potential effects of the action.[79] If the acting federal agency determines that a project may adversely affect a listed species or critical habitat, formal consultation and preparation of a biological opinion are required.[80] The biological opinion contains a detailed analysis of the effects of the agency action and contains the final determination as to whether the proposed action is likely to jeopardize the species or destroy or adversely modify its critical habitat.[81] If review results in a jeopardy or adverse modification determination, the biological opinion must identify any "reasonable and prudent alternatives" that could allow the project to proceed.[82]

Projects that will result in a level of injury to a species or habitat that will fall short of jeopardizing survival may still be approved subject to certain terms.[83]

The agency may be allowed to take some individuals of a listed species without triggering penalties under the act. These incidental takings are to be described in a statement accompanying the biological opinion.[84] Takings allowed under the consultation process are deemed consistent with the ESA; thus, they are not subject to penalties under the act, and no authorization other than the Incidental Take Statement or permit is required.[85]

Similarly, non-government entities may take a listed species if they receive an Incidental Take Permit from either FWS for NMFS under section 10 of the ESA.[86] To qualify for such a permit, a party must prepare a habitat conservation plan, in which the applicant describes the steps it will take to monitor, minimize, and mitigate any impacts to the threatened species; alternative actions and why they are not being used; and any other necessary and appropriate measures imposed by FWS or NMFS.[87]

The MMPA prohibits, with certain exceptions, the taking of marine mammals in U.S. waters and by U.S. citizens on the high seas, as well as the importation of marine mammals and marine mammal products into the United States. The statute is jointly administered by the Department of Commerce (through NOAA/NMFS) and the Department of the Interior (through FWS).[88] Among the statutory exceptions to the moratorium is a provision allowing NMFS or FWS to authorize, for a period of not more than five consecutive years, the "incidental" taking of small numbers of marine mammals.[89] Such incidental takes may be authorized only upon a fmding that the take will have a negligible impact on the species or stock and will not have an unmitigable adverse impact on the availability of the species or stock for taking for subsistence purposes by Alaskan natives as authorized by other sections of the MMPA.[90]

The regulations establish procedures for administering the MMPA, including application for authorization for incidental take of small numbers of marine mammals.[91] These regulations set forth the procedures for submission of requests for such authorization to the NMFS or FWS, standards for review, and the form of the authorization.[92]

The MBTA is the domestic law that implements U.S. obligations under separate treaties with Canada, Japan, Mexico, and Russia for the protection of migratory birds.[93] The MBTA generally prohibits the taking, killing, possession, or transportation of, and trafficking in, migratory birds, their eggs, parts, and nests.[94] Like the ESA, the general ban on taking protected birds can be waived under certain circumstances. Pursuant to section 704, the Secretary of the Interior is authorized to determine if, and by what means, the taking of migratory birds should be allowed.[95] FWS is responsible for permitting activities that would otherwise violate the MBTA. Its regulations at 50 C.F.R. § 21 make exceptions from permitting requirements for various purposes and provide for several specific types of permits, such as import and export permits, banding and marking permits, and scientific collection permits.[96] More general permits for special uses are also provided for under the regulations, although an applicant must make "a sufficient showing of benefit to the migratory bird resource, important research reasons, reasons of human concern for individual birds, or other compelling justification."[97]

It appears that FWS has not set MBTA regulations specific to the sort of unintentional harm caused by the rotating turbines of wind energy projects; thus, it is not clear that the permitting process under current regulations is immediately applicable to wind energy projects.[98] The FWS has, however, adopted voluntary, interim guidelines for minimizing the wildlife impacts from wind energy turbines.[99] As these guidelines indicate, compliance does not shield a company from prosecution for MBTA violations; however, "the Office of Law Enforcement and Department of Justice have used enforcement and prosecutorial discretion in the past regarding individuals, companies, or agencies who have made good faith efforts to avoid the incidental take of migratory birds."[100]

Many other federal and state statutes and regulations are applicable during consideration of permitting of offshore wind projects. The proposed Cape Wind project provides a useful example of the continuing role of other laws and regulations in the offshore wind permitting process. Cape Wind Associates, the private company that has proposed the project, has been seeking authorization since 2001. Cape Wind Associates originally sought federal siting approval from the Army Corps of Engineers pursuant to section 10 of the Rivers and Harbors Act, as described above. Environmental concerns delayed the permitting process. When EPAct transferred the offshore wind permitting authority to MMS/BOEMRE, Cape Wind Associates sought a permit from MMS for Cape Wind in accordance with EPAct. After environmental review was conducted by MMS pursuant to the requirements of NEPA, a fmal Environmental Impact Statement was published in January of 2009. On April 28, 2010, MMS issued a Record of Decision describing the decision to offer a commercial lease for the construction and operation of the proposed Cape Wind facility.[101]

Conclusion

Interest in developing offshore wind energy resources continues to grow, and projects are already in the initial stages of development. The United States has been developing the legal and regulatory framework to manage the issuance of permits for offshore development in its territorial sea and on the Outer Continental Shelf The OCSLA, as amended by EPAct 2005, provides DOI with authority to grant offshore property interests for the purpose of wind energy development (exercised through BOEMRE). Additional laws that predate the enactment of EPAct 2005 continue in force and also appear likely to remain a source of regulation, despite the apparent primary authority granted to DOI. Further, states also may claim a role in the permitting of offshore wind energy development pursuant to authorities granted under existing federal law.

End Notes

[1] See Mass. Tech. Collaborative, U.S. Dep't of Energy, & General Electric, A Framework for Offshore Wind Energy Development in the United States at 9 (September 2005); U.S. Dep't of Energy & U.S. Dep't of the Interior, White House Report in Response to the National Energy Policy Recommendations to Increase Renewable Energy Production on Federal Lands at 6 (August 2002).

[2] American Wind Energy Association, *AFfIE'A Year End 2009 Market Report, available* at http://www.awea.org/ publications/reports/4Q09.pdf.

[3] For an overview of offshore wind farm regulation in the United Kingdom, see Nathanael D. Hartland, The Wind and the Waves: Regulatory Uncertainty and Offshore Wind Power in the United States and United Kingdom, 24 U. Pa. J. Intl Econ. L. 691 (2003).

[4] Betsie Blumberg, Wind Farms: An Emerging Dilemma for East Coast National Parks, in National Park Service, Natural Resource Year in Review-2003 63 (March 2004); see Texas General Land Office, Offshore Wind Energy (available at *http://www.glo.stateix.us/news/ archive/2005/events/offshorewind.html).*

[5] For a discussion of policy and other issues related to wind energy, see CRS Report RL34546, *Wind Power in the United States: Technology, Economic, and Policy Issues,* by Stan Mark Kaplan.

[6] P.L. 109-58.

[7] Proc. No. 5928 (December 27, 1988).

[8] United Nations Convention on the Law of the Sea, December 10, 1982, 21 I.L.M. 1261 (entered into force November 16, 1994).

[9] UNCLOS arts. 2.1, 2.2, 3; see also United States v. California, 332 U.S. 19 (1947); Alabama v. Texas, 347 U.S. 272, 273-274 (1954).

[10] See United States v. California, 436 U.S. 32, 36 (1978); United States v. Alaska, 422 U.S. 184, 199 (1975); Alabama v. Texas, 347 U.S. 272, 273-274 (1954); United States v. California, 332 U.S. 19 (1947).

[11] UNCLOS art. 33.

[12] 43 U.S.C. §§ 1301-1303, 1311-1315.

[13] *Id.* at § 1301(a)(2). State jurisdiction typically extends 3 nautical miles (approximately 3.3 miles) seaward of the coast or "baseline." Texas and the Gulf Coast of Florida have jurisdiction over an area extending 3 "marine leagues" (9 nautical miles) from the baseline. 43 U.S.C. § 1301(a)(2).

[14] *Id.* at §§ 1314(a), 1311(a)(2).

[15] */d.* at § 1302.

[16] 16 U.S.C. §§ 1451-1464.

[17] Coastal U.S. states and territories, including the Great Lakes states, are eligible to receive federal assistance for their coastal zone management programs. Currently, there are 33 approved state and territorial plans. Of eligible states, only Illinois does not have an approved program. See National Oceanic and Atmospheric Administration, Office of Ocean and Coastal Resource Management, State and Territory Coastal Management Program Summaries, available at http://coastalmanagement.noaa.gov/mystate/welcome.html.

[18] */d.* at § 1452(1), (2).

[19] */d.* at § 1455(d)(2), (9)-(12).

[20] *Id.* at § 1455(d)(16).

[21] *Id. at §* 1456(c).

[22] /d.; Sec'y of the Interior v. California, 464 U.S. 312, 315 (1984).

[23] 16 U.S.C. § 1455(d)(11).

[24] See Rusty Russell, Neither Out Far Nor In Deep: The Prospects for Utility-Scale Wind Power in the Coastal Zone, 31 B.C. Envtl. Aff. L. Rev. 221, 240-241 (2004).

[25] E.g., Freshwater Wetlands Protection Act, N.J.S.A. 13:9B; Flood Hazard Area Control Act, N.J.S.A. 58:16A; Wetlands Act of 1970, N.J.S.A. 13:9A; Waterfront Development Act, N.J.S.A. 12:5-3; NJ Water Pollution Control Act, N.J.S.A. 58:10A; Coastal Area Facility Review Act (CAFRA), N.J.S.A. 13:19; Tidelands Act, N.J.S.A. 12:3.

[26] Russell, supra note 27, at 241.

[27] */d.* at App. E.

[28] Several federal laws would appear to indicate that Congress intends the OCS to be used only when permission has been expressly granted. See 43 U.S.C. § 1332(1), (3) ("the subsoil and seabed of the outer Continental Shelf appertain to the United States and are subject to its jurisdiction, control, and power of disposition.... "); see also 42 U.S.C. § 9101(a)(1) (stating that the purpose of the Ocean Thermal Energy Conversion Act is to "authorize and regulate the construction, location, ownership, and operation of ocean thermal energy conversion facilities.").

[29] 43 U.S.C. §§ 1701 et seq.

[30] 33 U.S.C. §§ 407-687. Section 10 was enacted in 1899, and its text has not changed substantively since that time. It states:

The creation of any obstruction not affirmatively authorized by Congress, to the navigable capacity of any of the waters of the United States is prohibited; and it shall not be lawful to build or commence the building of any wharf, pier, dolphin, boom, weir, breakwater, bulkhead, jetty, or other structures in any port, roadstead, haven, harbor, canal, navigable river, or other water of the United States, outside established harbor lines, or where no harbor lines have been established, except on plans recommended by the Chief of Engineers and authorized by the Secretary of the Army; and it shall not be lawful to excavate or fill, or in any manner to alter or modify the course, location, condition, or capacity of, any port, roadstead, haven, harbor, canal, lake, harbor or refuge, or enclosure within the limits of any breakwater, or of the channel of any navigable water of the United States, unless the work has been recommended by the Chief of Engineers and authorized by the Secretary of the Army prior to beginning the same. 33 U.S.C. § 403.

[31] 43 U.S.C. §§ 1331-1356a.

[32] 33 U.S.C. § 403. Corps regulations define the "navigable waters of the United States" as "those waters that are subject to the ebb and flow of the tide and/or are presently used, or have been used in the past, or may be susceptible for use to transport interstate or foreign

commerce." 33 C.F.R. § 329.4. Under the RHA, navigable waters "includes only those ocean and coastal waters that can be found up to three geographic miles seaward of the coast." Alliance To Protect Nantucket Sound, Inc. v. U.S. Dept of Army, 288 F.Supp.2d 64, 72 (D.Mass. 2003) (hereinafter Alliance I), aff'd, 398 F.3d 105 (1s[1] 2005) (hereinafter Alliance II); see also 33 C.F.R. § 329.12(a). On the OCS, however, the Corps' regulatory jurisdiction extends beyond that three-mile limit for certain purposes. 43 U.S.C. § 1333(a)(1), (e).

[33] 43 U.S.C. § 1337(p)(1). DOI authority to grant leases, easements, or rights-of-way on the OCS is contingent upon the permitted activities being consistent with the purposes specified by the law. The relevant property interest may only be issued if the OCS activity will:
(A)support exploration, development, production, or storage of oil or natural gas, except that a lease, easement, or right-of-way shall not be granted in an area in which oil and gas preleasing, leasing, and related activities are prohibited by a moratorium;
(B)support transportation of oil or natural gas, excluding shipping activities;
(C)produce or support production, transportation, or transmission of energy from sources other than oil and gas; or
(D)use, for energy-related purposes or for other authorized marine-related purposes, facilities currently or previously used for activities authorized under ... [the OCLSA], except that any oil and gas energy-related uses shall not be authorized in areas in which oil and gas preleasing, leasing, and related activities are prohibited by a moratorium. EPAct, § 388(a), adding new 43 U.S.C. § 1337(p)(1)(A)-(D).

[34] The April 2009 MOU referenced in the text originally confirmed the exclusive jurisdiction of the Minerals Management Service (MMS) over the described projects. BOEMRE was created in June 2010 as a successor agency to MMS. Department of the Interior Secretarial Order No. 3302, *Change of the Name of the Minerals Management Service to the Bureau of Ocean Energy Management, Regulation, and Enforcement* (June 18, 2010). Thus the jurisdiction of MMS agreed to in the April 2009 MOU was transferred to BOEMRE in June of 2010. Similarly, many of the rulemakings or other administrative actions taken by MMS as described in this memorandum now authorize activity by or assert the jurisdiction of BOEMRE as the successor agency to MMS.

[35] Id. at § 1337(p)(9).

[36] NEPA and its role in the offshore wind permitting process are discussed *infra* in the subsection entitled "Additional Laws and Regulations of Note."

[37] Id. at § 1337(p)(1).

[38] Id. at § 1337(p)(4).

[39] Id. at § 1337(p)(2)(A).

[40] *Id.* at § 1337(p)(3).

[41] Id. at § 1337(p)(5).

[42] *Id.* at § 1337(p)(2)(B).

[43] *Id*

[44] 43 U.S.C. § 1337(p)(4). MMS also appears to have adopted this interpretation in a rulemaking, stating that "MMS interprets the authority granted in section 388(a) of the Energy Policy Act of 2005 to issue leases, easements or rightsof-way as also providing MMS authority to regulate or permit the activities that occur on those leases, easements or rights-of-way, if those activities are energy related." 70 Fed. Reg. 77345, 77346 (December 30, 2005).

[45] 43 U.S.C. § 1337(p)(6).

[46] *Id*

[47] *Id.* at § 1337(p)(7).

[48] EPAct, § 388(e).

[49] 74 Fed. Reg. 19,638 (April 29, 2009).

[50] *See supra* fn. 34.

[51] *Id* at 19,647.

[52] *Id.*

[53] *Id.* at 19,678-19,682.
[54] *Id.* at 19,678.
[55] *Id*
[56] *Id*
[57] *id.*
[58] *Id*
[59] *Id*
[60] *Id.*
[61] *Id.*
[62] *Id.*
[63] *Id*
[64] See, e.g., Minerals Management Service, "MMS and Virginia Hold Offshore Renewable Energy Task Force Meeting," press release, December 8, 2009, *http://www.mms.gov/ooc/press/2009/press1209.htm;* Minerals Management Service, "MMS and Massachusetts Hold Offshore Renewable Energy Task Force Meeting," press release, November 19, 2009, http://www.boemre.gov/ooc/press/2009/press1119.htm. MMS issued similar press releases regarding meetings with other coastal states.
[65] *Id*
[66] *Memorandum of Understanding Between the Department of the Interior U.S. Minerals Management Service and the Department of the Interior U.S. Fish and Wildlife Service Regarding Implementation of Executive Order 13186, "Responsibilities of Federal Agencies to Protect Migratory Birds,"* June 4, 2009.
[67] *Id.*
[68] 43 U.S.C. § 1337(p)(9).
[69] 42 U.S.C. §§ 4321 et seq.
[79] 40 C.F.R. § 1508.4.
[71] See U.S. Army Corps Of Eng'rs, Environmental Impact Statement: Scope of Work, Wind Power Facility Proposed by Cape Wind Associates, LLC 3, available at http://www.nae.usace.army.mil/projects/ma/ccwf/windscope.pdf. See also United States v. Alaska, 503 U.S. 569, 579-580 (1992) (holding that Corps permitting decisions under section 10 are not limited to considerations of navigation).
[72] 16 U.S.C. §§ 1531-1544.
[73] 16 U.S.C. §§ 1361-1407.
[74] 16 U.S.C. §§ 703-712.
[75] Under the ESA, species are listed as either "endangered" or "threatened" based on the risk of their extinction. An "endangered" species is "any species which is in danger of extinction throughout all or a significant portion of its range." A "threatened" species is "any species which is likely to become an endangered species within the foreseeable future throughout all or a significant portion of its range." 16 U.S.C. §§ 1532(6), (20).
[76] 16 U.S.C. § 1532(19).
[77] *Id.* at § 1536(a)(2).
[78] 50 C.F.R. § 402.12(c). It should also be noted that some protections also attach to "candidate" species, i.e., those proposed but not officially listed. Under current law, an agency must "confer" with the appropriate Secretary if agency action will likely jeopardize the continued existence of any candidate species or adversely modify critical habitat proposed for designation. This is distinct from the section 7 consultation process, less formal, and meant to assist planning early in the process should the species be listed and more definite protections attach. See 16 U.S.C. § 1536(a)(4); 50 C.F.R. § 402.10.
[79] 50 C.F.R. § 402.12(b), (d).
[80] *Id* at § 402.14(e).
[81] *Id.* at § 402.14(h).
[82] *Id.* at § 402.14(h)(3).
[83] *Id* at § 402.14(i).

[84] *Id.* at § 402.14(i)(1)(i)-(v).

[85] 16 U.S.C. § 1536(b)(4); 50 C.F.R. § 402.14(i)(5).

[86] 16 U.S.C. 1539.

[87] 50 C.F.R. § 17.32(b)(1) (for FWS); 50 C.F.R. § 222.307(b)(5) (for NMFS).

[88] The statute defines *Secretary* as the Secretary of the department in which NOAA is operating (Commerce) for purposes of regulation related to all members of the order Cetacea (whales and porpoises) and all members, except walruses, of the order Pinnipedia (seals). The statute defines *Secretary* as Secretary of the Interior (operating through the FWS) with respect to all other marine mammals (manatees, dugongs, polar bears, sea otters, and walruses). 16 U.S.C. § 1362(12)(A).

[89] 16 U.S.C. § 1371(5)(A).

[90] 16 U.S.C. § 1371(5)(A)(i).

[91] 50 C.F.R. § 18.27 (FWS regulations); 50 C.F.R. Part 216, Subpart I (NMFS regulations).

[92] *Id.*

[93] Birds that receive protection under the MBTA are listed at 50 C.F.R. § 10.13.

[94] 16 U.S.C. § 703.

[95] 16 U.S.C. § 704.

[96] 50 C.F.R. §§ 21.11-21.26.

[97] Id. at § 21.27.

[98] See 69 Fed. Reg. 31074 (June 2, 2004) ("Current regulations authorize permits for take of migratory birds for activities such as scientific research, education, and depredation control. However, these regulations do not expressly address the issuance of permits for incidental take.").

[99] U.S. Fish and Wildlife Service, Interim Guidance on Avoiding and Minimizing Wildlife Impacts from Wind Turbines, (May 2003) (available at http://www.fws.gov/habitatconservation/wind.pdf).

[100] *Id.* at 2.

[101] *MMS, Record of Decision, Cape Wind Energy Project, Horseshoe Shoal, Nantucket Sound,* April 28, 2010. Available at http://www.doi.gov/news/doinews/upload/Cape-Wind-ROD.pdf.

CHAPTER SOURCES

Chapter 1 - This is an edited, reformatted and augmented version of a Congressional Research Service publication, R40806, dated September 8th, 2009.

Chapter 2 - This is an edited, reformatted and augmented version of a U.S. International Trade Commission publication, RL33404, dated September 20th, 2010.

Chapter 3 - This is an edited, reformatted and augmented version of a U.S. International Trade Commission publication, R40175, dated September 3rd, 2009.

Index

A

B

C

D

M

N

O

P

Q

R

S

T

V

W

Y